CLEVER CODING

INCREDIBLE MACHINES

EXTRAORDINARY INVENTIONS

ENGINEERING

for Curious Kids

An illustrated introduction to
building machines and amazing structures!

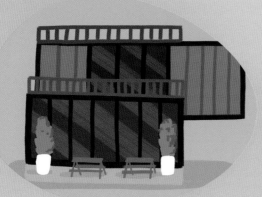

BUILDING THE FUTURE

SUPER STRUCTURES

ARCTURUS

ARCTURUS

This edition published in 2022 by Arcturus Publishing Limited
26/27 Bickels Yard, 151–153 Bermondsey Street,
London SE1 3HA

Author: Chris Oxlade
Illustrator: Alex Foster
Consultant: David Baker
Designer: Dani Leigh
Editors: Becca Clunes, William Potter

ISBN: 978-1-3988-2018-0
CH010028US
Supplier 29, Date 0722, PI 00000999

Printed in China

What is STEM?

STEM is a world-wide initiative that aims to cultivate an interest in
Science, Technology, Engineering, and Mathematics, in an effort to
promote these disciplines to as wide a variety of students as possible.

CONTENTS

WELCOME TO THE WORLD OF ENGINEERING

Skyscrapers, bridges, cars, trains, ships, phones, computers, game consoles, robots, replacement limbs, oil refineries, and drugs—these are just a tiny fraction of the amazing things that come from the world of engineering.

The word *engineer* comes from the Latin word *ingenium*, which means cleverness. Engineers know a lot about science and mathematics, and use their knowledge to solve engineering problems. An engineer might work out how build a bridge over a river, or make a robot to pick crops on a farm, or design a machine to put icing on cakes.

Turn the pages and take a journey through the world of engineering. You'll discover how engineering began, some famous events and people from the history of engineering, how engineers work today, and the main types of engineering—civil engineering, mechanical engineering, electrical and electronic engineering, and chemical engineering. What kind of engineer would you be?

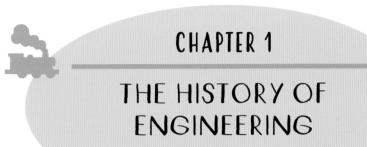

CHAPTER 1

THE HISTORY OF ENGINEERING

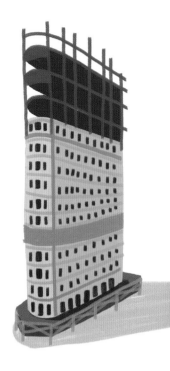

Engineering is old—older than you might think. Its history stretches back for thousands of years. So, who were the first engineers? They were probably hunter-gatherers who crafted simple tools from stone and wood, choosing and working with materials as modern-day engineers do.

Engineering on a giant scale began in ancient times with the Egyptians, Greeks, and Romans. It took a big leap forward during the Industrial Revolution with iron, steel, steam, and the launch of industries. Many new branches of engineering have sprung up in the last hundred years. Read on to find out about the engineers of the past...

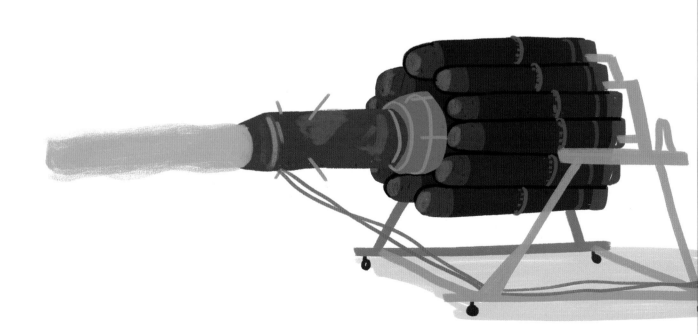

ANCIENT ENGINEERING

The giant stone pyramids of Egypt show us that skilled civil engineers were at work more than four-and-a-half thousand years ago. Later, the engineers of Ancient Rome became experts at constructing roads, monumental buildings, and military machinery.

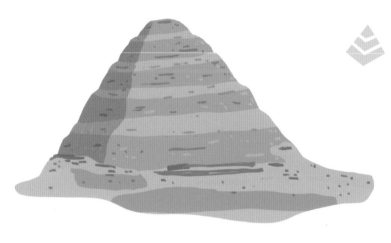

PYRAMID BUILDERS

The Egyptian pyramids may look like simple structures, but their construction required skills such as accurate measuring and careful stone cutting. The earliest pyramids had steps rather than smooth, sloping sides. An example is the Step Pyramid of Djoser, which was built around 2650 BCE. The pyramid was probably designed and built by an Egyptian engineer named Imhotep, one of the first engineers we know about.

ROMAN ROAD ENGINEERS

The Ancient Romans built a network of roads that stretched across their vast empire. The roads were vital for moving troops and goods. Roman engineers built their roads in straight lines whenever they could. They invented an instrument called a **groma** for marking the route that a new road would follow. The groma included plumb bobs (lead weights on strings), so that an engineer could check that a staff was upright. Looking along the arms allowed stick markers to be lined up accurately.

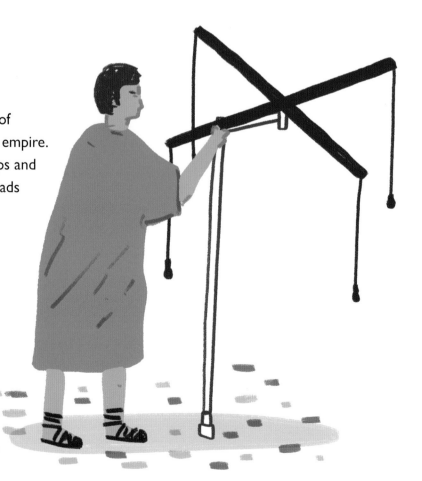

OUT OF CURIOSITY

The Pyramid of Khufu (also called the Great Pyramid of Giza) in Egypt was 146 m (481 ft) tall on completion in 2465 BCE. The sides are 230 m (760 ft) long and accurate to within 5 cm (2 in).

 # DOME STRUCTURE

In ancient times, engineers lacked the materials that modern engineers can use, especially steel that we use for wide roofs or bridge spans. Roman engineers did have a form of concrete, made from volcanic ash, lime, and gravel. They were expert at using concrete in place of stone to form arches and domes. The Pantheon in Rome was the world's first concrete dome and is still standing today.

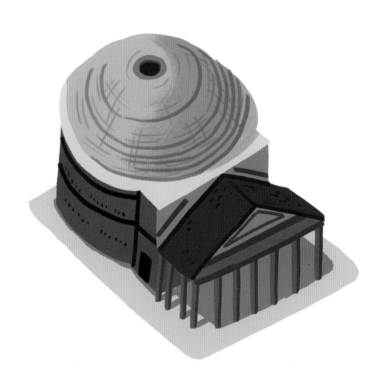

BUILDING MACHINES

Roman engineers understood simple machines such as levers, pulleys, wheels, and **axles**, and used them in cranes for lifting heavy building materials. More than a thousand years later, medieval engineers used similar machinery to help build magnificent cathedrals—the tallest buildings of the time.

THE INDUSTRIAL REVOLUTION

Around 250 years ago, the way of life in Britain, Western Europe, and the United States started to change. Populations grew quickly, and industries began. People moved from the countryside into the cities to work in factories. This period is known as the Industrial Revolution, and engineers made it happen.

STEAM POWER

During the eighteenth century, the demand for coal and metal ores grew. Deep digging was difficult because of flooding. In 1712, English engineer Thomas Newcomen found a solution. He invented a steam engine called the atmospheric engine, which pumped water out of mines. Hundreds of these engines were installed. Newcomen's engine design was greatly improved in the 1760s by Scottish engineer James Watt. His engines were smaller and used less coal. They were soon powering factory machinery, too.

TEXTILE MILLS

Before the Industrial Revolution, the production of textiles such as wool and cotton cloth was a "cottage industry"—the textiles were made by individual craftspeople at home. Then, mechanical engineers invented machines to perform the processes in textile production, such as spinning machines to make thread and powered looms to weave thread into cloth. Textile-mill machinery was first powered by flowing water before steam power took over.

CUTTING SCREWS

An important step in the history of mechanical engineering was interchangeability—this meant making parts for machines accurately enough that a particular part could be taken off one machine and used on another machine of the same type. English engineer Henry Maudsley helped by inventing a screw-cutting lathe around 1797. His machine cut the spiral threads on bolts very accurately. Before this, nuts and bolts were not guaranteed to fit together!

SHAPING METALS

Machines used for cutting and shaping materials are known as machine tools. Mechanical engineers developed various machine tools, such as saws, drills, **lathes**, and milling machines. Machine tools could make the parts for machines, or furniture, or weapons, more accurately and more quickly than traditional craftspeople. American engineer Eli Whitney invented the first milling machine, which shapes metal by cutting away material.

ON THE MOVE

One of main advances of the Industrial Revolution was the large-scale production of iron. Along with the steam engine, iron transformed long-distance transportation, making it faster and more convenient. Engineers designed ships with iron hulls that were driven by steam, and steam locomotives to pull trains along iron rails.

BIGGER AND BETTER SHIPS

During the nineteenth century, engineers started to build ships from iron instead of wood. Iron was much stronger and could be shaped into girders, plates, and other shapes, allowing engineers to create ships much larger than before. This enabled them to carry many more passengers and much more cargo. Steam power allowed ships to continue moving when sailing ships were stranded due to lack of wind. The *Great Eastern* steamship, launched in 1854, was built by British engineer Isambard Kingdom Brunel.

ISAMBARD KINGDOM BRUNEL

One of the most famous civil engineers of all time, Isambard Kingdom Brunel built oceangoing ships, including the *Great Eastern*, railroads, bridges, and tunnels. His first ship was the *Great Western*, the first steamship to carry passengers regularly across the Atlantic. He planned the route of a train service from London to Bristol in England, including its many stations, bridges, and tunnels. His ingenious bridge designs enabled carriages and trains to cross wide rivers and deep canyons.

?

OUT OF CURIOSITY

Brunel's giant ship the *Great Eastern* measured 211 m (692 ft) from bow to stern. That's as long as two soccer fields end to end. It was the largest ship ever built at the time.

TRACKS AND TRAINS

During the nineteenth century, engineers constructed thousands of miles of rail lines in Europe and North America. The rail lines made travel between towns and cities much faster—previously, people had to walk or ride in horse-drawn coaches on rough roads. One of the greatest achievements was the Pacific Railroad. This line, built in the 1860s, stretched 3,075 km (1,911 mi) across North America, linking the east and west coasts. One of the greatest challenges for the engineers was to choose the best route through the mountains that would keep the number of bridges and tunnels to a minimum.

BRIDGES AND TUNNELS

As networks of roads, rail lines, and canals grew rapidly during the nineteenth century, engineers invented new types of bridges to cross wide rivers and deep valleys. They also learned how to tunnel under hills, mountains, and rivers.

BUILDING LONG

For many hundreds of years, the only permanent type of bridge was the stone arch. Thousands of these bridges are still in use today, but stone arches could not be built

long enough to stretch over wide, deep rivers. Engineers turned to iron and steel, and invented new types of bridges. They built iron and steel arches, iron and steel beams, and suspension bridges supported by iron chains or steel cables. The Brooklyn Bridge in New York, completed in 1883, was one of the first suspension bridges.

DIGGING TUNNELS THROUGH ROCK

Digging tunnels through mountains was a difficult engineering problem. Digging by hand was too slow, so engineers turned to explosives. Drilling machines were developed to bore holes in the tunnel face, into which explosive charges were placed. The 14-km (8-mi) Mont Cenis Tunnel links France and Italy. Opened in 1871 after 14 years of drilling and blasting, it was the first tunnel in which engineers used dynamite.

TUNNELS UNDERWATER

Digging tunnels through soft rocks under rivers gave engineers a new set of problems. It was very risky because of the chance that the roof and walls might collapse, causing flooding. The answer was a shield, which was invented by French engineer Marc Isambard Brunel, father of Isambard Kingdom Brunel. The shield supported the ground as workers dug away at the tunnel face.

 # LEARNING THE HARD WAY

Engineers didn't always get things right. Their mistakes sometimes led to disasters, but they taught them valuable lessons. One disaster struck the Tay Bridge in Scotland in 1879. The bridge collapsed as a train crossed it during a violent storm. Tragically, the bridge had not been designed to withstand strong side winds.

ENGINEERING NEW CITIES

The rapid growth of cities in the nineteenth century caused problems that engineers had to solve. Housing was cramped and unhygienic because of lack of fresh water supplies and sewers. Then, as businesses grew in the heart of cities, transportation was needed to help workers get around.

BUILDING UPWARD

For tall buildings constructed using stone or brick, the walls on the lower floors need to be very thick to support the walls above. It's not practical to build very tall office or apartment buildings this way. Toward the end of the nineteenth century, civil engineers began to erect tall buildings with strong steel frames to support them instead. One of the first was the Flatiron Building in New York City, with 22 floors. It was completed in 1902.

GOING UNDERGROUND

 As the population of cities grew, people started to travel to work in huge numbers. Engineers had to come up with ways of moving everyone around quickly and efficiently. In some cities, the best solution was to avoid the bustling streets and go underground. This meant digging tunnels and building subway stations. The first "underground railway" was opened in London in 1863, with trains pulled by steam locomotives.

DELIVERING CLEAN WATER

Unpleasant and life-threatening diseases, such as cholera, were common in the growing cities of the nineteenth century. The diseases spread easily because of the lack of clean water and because human waste was washed into streams and rivers. City authorities employed engineers to build dams outside the cities to store fresh water, and systems of pipes and aqueducts, such as New York's Harlem High Bridge, to bring the water into the cities. They also installed sewers to take away wastewater and treatment plants to clean it.

WORKING WITH CHEMICALS

The growth of cities and industries in the nineteenth century created a demand for chemicals. These included fuels for lighting and heating, the chemicals needed for making materials such as glass, and chemicals for agriculture. This led to a new branch of engineering—chemical engineering.

THE FATHER OF CHEMICAL ENGINEERING

British chemist George E. Davis was one of the first chemical engineers. He designed and built several chemical factories in England. He also worked as an inspector in soda-ash factories, making sure that not too much acid was pumped into the atmosphere. Later, he became a lecturer in chemical engineering in Manchester, England, and in 1887 published the *Handbook of Chemical Engineering*, the first book about the chemical processes used in factories.

SOLVAY'S SODA-ASH PLANT

Soda ash (chemical name: sodium carbonate) is an important raw material in the manufacture of glass and other chemicals. Originally, soda ash came from natural sources, but high demand meant that **synthetic** soda ash was needed. In Belgium, Ernest Solvay and his team of chemists invented a process for making soda ash. In 1877, they opened a huge chemical plant to make soda ash for the local glassmaking industry.

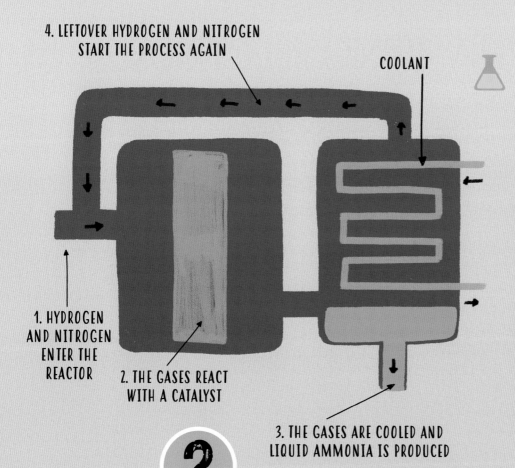

4. LEFTOVER HYDROGEN AND NITROGEN START THE PROCESS AGAIN

COOLANT

1. HYDROGEN AND NITROGEN ENTER THE REACTOR

2. THE GASES REACT WITH A CATALYST

3. THE GASES ARE COOLED AND LIQUID AMMONIA IS PRODUCED

AMMONIA FOR CROPS

As the world's population grew through the nineteenth century and early twentieth century, more and more food was needed to feed everyone. Chemical engineers helped by making artificial fertilizers. Ammonia was a vital ingredient for fertilizer. A process for making it was developed by two German chemists named Fritz Haber and Carl Bosch. The process is now called the Haber-Bosch process. Large-scale production began in 1910.

OUT OF CURIOSITY

It's said that if the Haber-Bosch process had not been invented to make ammonia for fertilizers, the world's population would be just half of what it is today!

OIL FOR LIGHT

Chemical engineers learned how to extract useful products from coal and petroleum using a chemical process called **distillation**. One of these products was called kerosene, which was burned in oil lamps to light mines and homes. Kerosene was a popular fuel for lamps until the early twentieth century, when oil lamps began to be replaced by electric lighting.

UNDERSTANDING ELECTRICITY

Today, we rely on electricity and electronics to power machines at home and in factories, and gadgets such as phones and tablets. Electrical engineering began after scientists discovered how to store and control electricity. Electrical engineers applied the science to make electricity work for us.

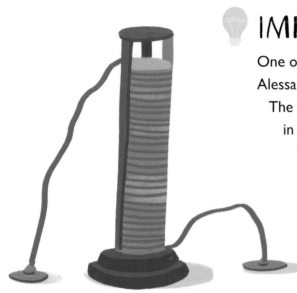

IMPORTANT DISCOVERIES

One of the earliest discoveries was made by the Italian Alessandro Volta, who built the very first battery in 1800. The battery contained disks of zinc and copper placed in a pile, separated by paper disks soaked in salt water. Two vital discoveries for communications came from physicists James Clerk Maxwell and Heinrich Hertz. Maxwell realized that radio waves and light are forms of **electromagnetic radiation**. German Heinrich Hertz proved Maxwell's theory by producing and detecting radio waves.

POWER FOR PEOPLE

The famous American inventor and engineer Thomas Edison was one of the first electrical engineers. In 1882, Edison opened the first commercial electricity generating station in the United States. The plant, called the Pearl Street Station, supplied electricity to Manhattan in New York, powering thousands of light bulbs. Inside were **generators** powered by steam that produced the electricity.

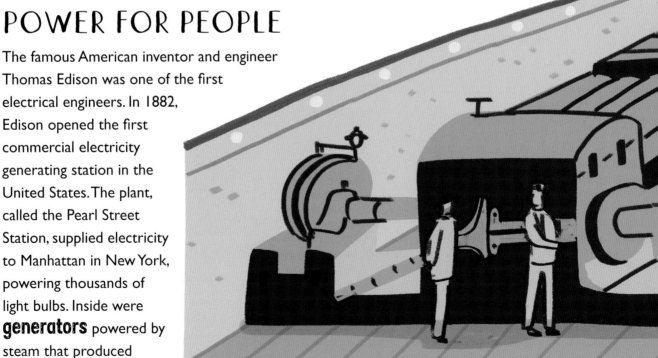

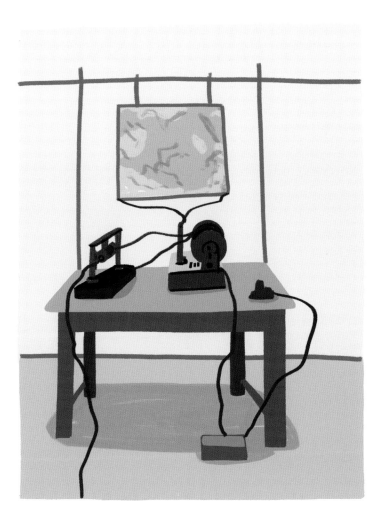

RADIO COMMUNICATIONS

Italian scientist and engineer Guglielmo Marconi followed up the work of Maxwell and Hertz by inventing wireless telegraphy. He designed transmitters to produce radio signals and receivers to detect the signals. At first, the signals reached across a room, but in 1899, he sent a telegraph message over 50 km (80 miles) from England to France, then in 1901 sent messages across the Atlantic Ocean. Marconi's work was a major step forward in communications engineering.

ELECTRONICS

In electronic circuits, the flow of electric current is directed by the components in the circuit. The first electronic devices were called **valves** and only worked inside glass tubes with a vacuum inside. Valves were used in radios and early computers. In 1947, engineers at Bell Laboratories in the United States invented the **transistor**, which used **semiconductors**. Transistors and similar devices replaced valves. Later, they were built on a microscopic scale on microchips. There can be several thousand of them in modern electronic devices.

ENGINEERING IN MEDICINE

Mechanical engineers began using their skills in the field of medicine. At first, they developed mechanical aids such as artificial limbs. As medical knowledge grew and surgical skills improved, engineers helped by designing medical equipment and even artificial organs.

REPLACEMENT LIMBS

Replacement arms or legs, now known as prosthetic limbs, were the earliest application of engineering in medicine. The idea was not new, since very simple artificial limbs were made in Ancient Egypt, but in the nineteenth century, the demand for artificial limbs grew quickly because of the number of soldiers losing limbs, especially during the American Civil War in the 1860s. At the time, amputation was the best way to save an injured soldier's life. This artificial leg from 1871 (right) has a hinged knee to make the lower leg swing naturally when walking.

AN ARTIFICIAL HEART

An artificial heart is a pump that takes the place of a patient's damaged or unhealthy heart. Normally, a patient is fitted with an artificial heart temporarily until a heart transplant is possible. The Jarvik-7 artificial heart was designed by American physician Robert Jarvik, and the first patient received one in 1982. It was made from aluminum and plastic. This design for an artificial heart turned out to be unsuccessful.

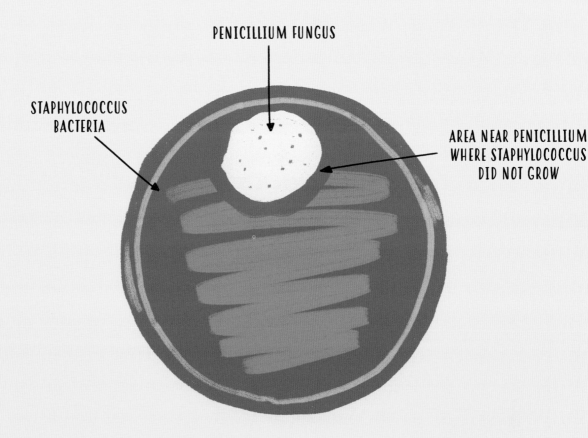

STAPHYLOCOCCUS BACTERIA

PENICILLIUM FUNGUS

AREA NEAR PENICILLIUM WHERE STAPHYLOCOCCUS DID NOT GROW

 # DESIGNING DRUGS

Engineering skills are also used to design and develop new drugs for treating diseases. Engineers in the field of biochemical engineering work with the complex chemicals that make up the human body. A major advance came during World War II with the large-scale manufacture of penicillin, which was the first antibiotic used to fight infections. This had been discovered by accident in 1928 in Britain by Alexander Fleming, but Fleming could find no way to manufacture it.

OUT OF CURIOSITY

Penicillin became available in 1944, a year before the end of World War II. In the final year of the war, it saved the lives of thousands of soldiers injured on the battlefield.

CARS, PLANES, AND ROCKETS

During the twentieth century, engineers designed and built cars, aircraft, and spacecraft. They invented new technologies, such as jet and rocket engines, and built factories to produce cars and aircraft. New branches of engineering emerged: auto engineering, aeronautical engineering, and aerospace engineering.

MASS PRODUCTION

Early cars, which were built at the end of the nineteenth century and the beginning of the twentieth, were made one by one in small factories. Production was slow, and the cars were expensive. Auto engineering took a big leap forward with mass production, where cars move along production lines with parts being added along the way. Mass production of the famous Model-T Ford began in 1908. The Model-T was designed to be built on a production line to keep costs down.

THE JET ENGINE

Since the first aircraft took off just over a hundred years ago, aeronautical engineers have been solving problems to make aircraft larger, faster, more reliable, and safer for us to fly in. They have designed new types of aircraft, new types of aero engines, and new ways of controlling aircraft. In the 1930s, British engineer Frank Whittle designed a jet engine to power fast aircraft after propeller engines had reached their speed limit. At first, his idea was not taken seriously. Whittle had to design his engine from scratch. His first **prototype** engine ran successfully in 1937.

ENGINEERING INTO SPACE

In the 1940s, a team of German engineers headed by Wernher von Braun developed a rocket weapon called the V2. This was the start of a new branch of engineering known as aerospace engineering. Von Braun's team had to design rocket engines and solve the problem of how to guide them through the air. Von Braun went on to work in the United States, where he developed rockets that could travel in orbit around the Earth. Working for NASA, he led the team that designed the giant Saturn V rocket that launched astronauts to the Moon in 1969.

CHAPTER 2

BEING AN ENGINEER

In this chapter, we'll look at what you need to know in order to be an engineer. For a start, you don't get to be an engineer without being good at mathematics and science—mathematics for measuring and doing calculations, and science for understanding how the world around us works. Engineers must study their own branch of engineering, too.

We'll also find out how engineers work from day to day. When engineers are given a problem, they follow steps to seek a solution in what's called the design process. They'll do a little brainstorming, a bit of sketching, and try a few things out. They might have to rethink things, but most of the time they'll find an answer eventually.

BRANCHES OF ENGINEERING

Today, the word *engineering* is used for a huge range of different jobs. There are four main fields, or branches, of engineering: civil engineering, mechanical engineering, electrical engineering, and chemical engineering.

The four main branches of engineering are shown on this tree. Many specialist types of engineering are outside these branches, such as biochemical engineering and software engineering (to do with programming computers). This book looks at the four main branches, one in each chapter.

MECHANICAL ENGINEERING

Mechanical engineering is designing machines and tools— that could be anything from a pair of scissors to an aircraft. Mechanical engineers work mainly with metals and know how to shape materials to make parts for machines. Mechanical engineers understand physics, mathematics, and materials science.

ELECTRICAL ENGINEERING

Electrical engineers design and build electrical and electronic circuits, from a simple doorbell to a complex tablet. They develop communications technology and automatic machines, including robots (along with mechanical engineers). Electrical engineers study mathematics and physics and are experts in electricity.

CIVIL ENGINEERING

Civil engineers build structures such as skyscrapers, bridges, tunnels, roads, and dams. They work with tough materials, such as steel and concrete, and powerful machinery including cranes and diggers. Civil engineers study physics, mathematics, and materials.

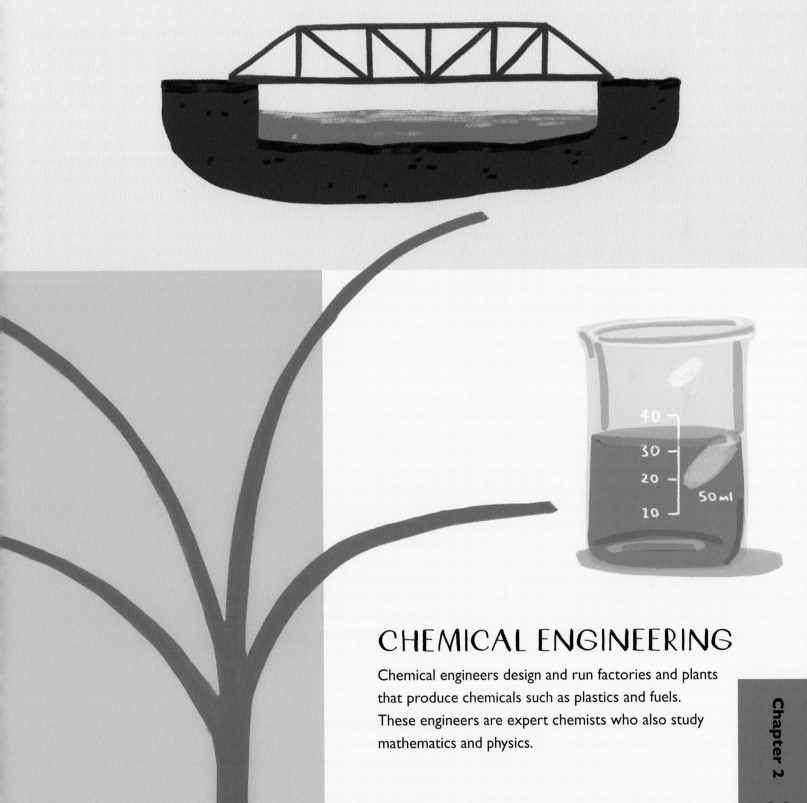

CHEMICAL ENGINEERING

Chemical engineers design and run factories and plants that produce chemicals such as plastics and fuels. These engineers are expert chemists who also study mathematics and physics.

Mathematics is one of the most important subjects for engineers—most engineering would be impossible to do without it. So, engineers need to study basic concepts, such as measuring and doing calculations, and more complicated ideas, such as calculus and statistics.

CAREFUL MEASUREMENTS

Measuring is a vital skill in engineering. An engineer might need to measure the length of a piece of machinery or find out the width of a road. Engineers also need to measure quantities such as speed, volume, the strength of a force, acidity, current, or voltage. A **caliper** is a tool that mechanical engineers use to measure small objects accurately, such as the length or width of a screw. A **theodolite** (left) is used by civil engineers for measuring angles and distances, often when measuring on a building site.

LARGE AND SMALL NUMBERS

Engineers need to understand the scale of the objects they are working with compared with the scale of everyday things, and how to measure and write down large and small numbers. For example, an engineer might use millimeters (or tenths of inches) to measure the width of a screw and meters (or feet) to measure the width of a building. Engineers show large and small quantities using powers and prefixes. For instance, *milli* (m) means one-thousandth, or 0.0001, also written 10^{-3}, so a millivolt = 1/1,000 volt.

NUMBER		POWER	PREFIX	SYMBOL
ONE BILLION	1,000,000,000	10^9	GIGA	G
ONE MILLION	1,000,000	10^6	MEGA	H
ONE THOUSAND	1,000	10^3	KILO	k
ONE	1	10^0	NONE	none
ONE-THOUSANDTH	0.001	10^{-3}	MILLI	m
ONE-MILLIONTH	0.000001	10^{-6}	MICRO	μ
ONE-BILLIONTH	0.000000001	10^{-9}	NANO	n
ONE-TRILLIONTH	0.000000000001	10^{-12}	PICO	P

Engineers need to know about two-dimensional and three-dimensional shapes, such as rectangles, circles, cubes, and spheres, and how to calculate the areas and volumes of these shapes. For example, a civil engineer might need to figure out the volume of a rectangular trench to find out how much concrete is needed to fill it, or a chemical engineer might need to figure out the dimensions of a container to hold a certain volume of liquid.

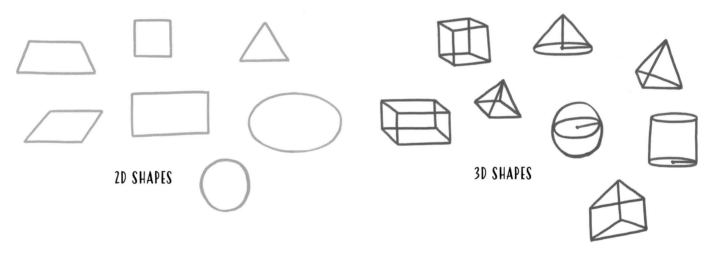

2D SHAPES

3D SHAPES

UNDERSTANDING GRAPHS

Engineers use graphs, charts, and tables to show how things are linked together. In electrical engineering, a **sine wave** (right) shows how the changing strength of an alternating current as time passes. Graphs, charts, and tables are also a useful way of making data easier to understand.

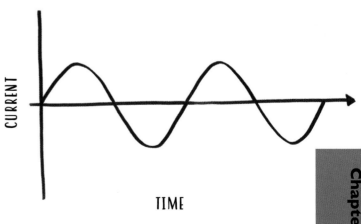

ENGINEERS AND SCIENCE

Engineers need a good all-round knowledge of the science in their own branch of engineering. Civil and mechanical engineers need to know about physics and materials, electrical engineers need to know about electricity, and chemical engineers need to be expert chemists, too.

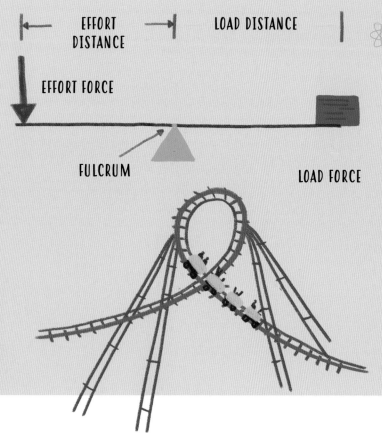

EFFORT DISTANCE

LOAD DISTANCE

EFFORT FORCE

FULCRUM

LOAD FORCE

FORCES AND MACHINES

A branch of physics called **mechanics** is the most important for civil engineers and mechanical engineers. Mechanics is all about forces, about how things move, and about simple machines such as **levers** and **pulleys**. It tells engineers how forces move, squash, or bend objects.

Some engineers must consider the affect of forces on people as well as materials. For instance, roller coaster engineers aim to create a thrilling ride without making the riders black out or feel sick.

CHEMISTRY

Chemical engineers need to have a good understanding of chemistry, so that they can design and build chemical plants. Chemicals can react together to form new chemicals or sometimes split apart to make new chemicals, so engineers need knowledge of chemical reactions. Engineers from other branches of engineering may need to understand chemistry, too.

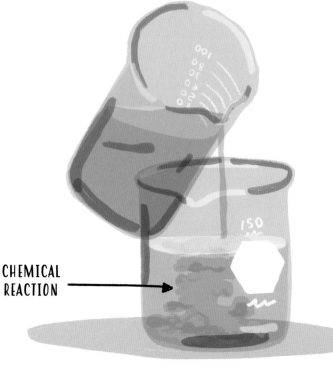

CHEMICAL REACTION

CIRCUIT DIAGRAM

⚛ ELECTRICITY

Electrical and electronic engineers use their knowledge of electricity to design and build electrical circuits for anything from power plants to game consoles. They need to understand how electric current flows, how electric and electronic components work, how to put components together to make circuits that do different jobs, and how to draw circuit diagrams to communicate their plans to other people.

⚛ ENERGY AND POWER

Nothing happens without some energy to make it happen, so engineers need to know all about energy and power (power is how quickly energy is transferred from one place to another). An electrical engineer designing a wind turbine would need to know how much power came from the turbine, and a chemical engineer might need to know the energy needed to make a chemical reaction happen in a chemical plant.

MATERIALS AND STRUCTURES

Mechanical engineers and civil engineers need knowledge of the properties of metals, plastics, ceramics, wood, and other materials used in their projects. They also need to know what shapes are strong enough not to bend or buckle.

THE PROPERTIES OF MATERIALS

Engineers need to be aware of the properties of different materials. Properties include elasticity (how easily a material stretches), density, hardness, electrical conductivity, and heat conductivity. Bicycle helmets have tough plastic shells with energy-absorbing foam inside, for example. Composite materials, such as the carbon-reinforced plastic of a bicycle frame, have the properties of different materials combined. Carbon-reinforced plastic is lightweight but extremely strong.

ASK A QUESTION

An engineer needs to know what the problem is before solving it. The first stage in the engineering process is always writing down a question that needs to be answered.

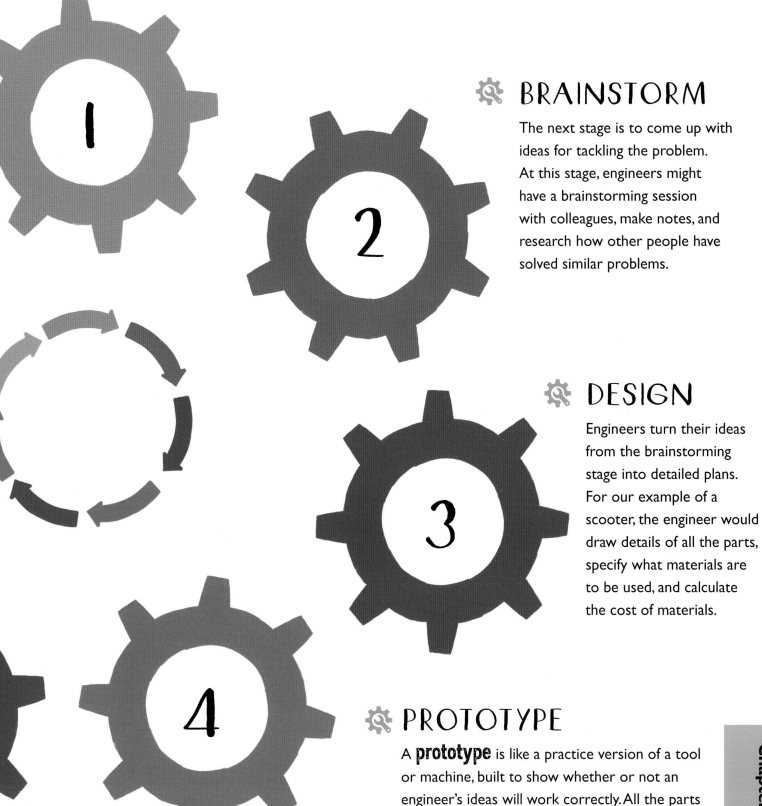

BRAINSTORM

The next stage is to come up with ideas for tackling the problem. At this stage, engineers might have a brainstorming session with colleagues, make notes, and research how other people have solved similar problems.

DESIGN

Engineers turn their ideas from the brainstorming stage into detailed plans. For our example of a scooter, the engineer would draw details of all the parts, specify what materials are to be used, and calculate the cost of materials.

PROTOTYPE

A **prototype** is like a practice version of a tool or machine, built to show whether or not an engineer's ideas will work correctly. All the parts are made following the plans and specifications.

THE DESIGN PROCESS

The first stage in the process is to define a problem that needs to be solved. For example, an engineer designing a child's scooter would need to know what features it needs, what size it needs to be, how heavy it can be, and the budget that can be spent.
Then, the engineer can start to design the scooter.

BRAINSTORMING

The next step in the design process is to gather ideas. Engineers talk to other people, such as other engineers, designers, architects, and scientists. They might meet up for a "brainstorming" session, where everybody has a chance to suggest ideas for discussion.

KNOWLEDGE AND EXPERIENCE

During the design process, engineers use their expert knowledge and the experience they have gained from working on similar projects. They also use intuition (a natural gift for understanding a subject) and their imagination. Finally, they do research into similar designs that exist, such as other gadgets, machines, and structures. Engineers also look at restraints, including cost, weight, time, and the difficulty of making something.

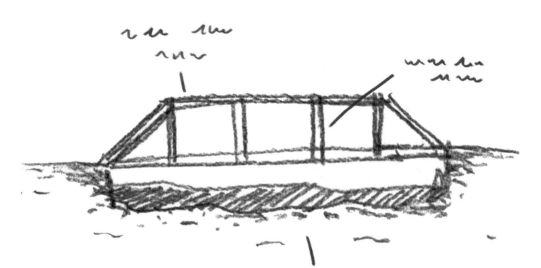

DESIGN IDEAS

With brainstorming and research complete, engineers bring all their ideas together and start designing. For gadgets, machines, and structures, sketching is an important stage in design. Sketching is a quick way of getting ideas down on paper and allows other people to see what the engineer is thinking. Engineers choose materials at this stage, too. Engineers normally sketch out several possibilities before choosing the best solution—the one that they will make a **prototype** for.

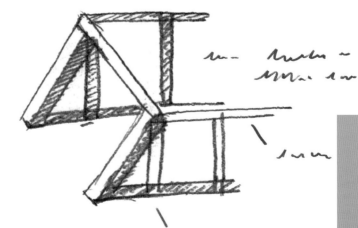

The word *prototype* means a thing that's copied to make other things. So, a prototype of a gadget, car, or rocket is the first version of that thing. Engineers build prototypes to test their ideas or to make sure that all the parts of a machine fit together correctly.

✔ TESTING, TESTING, TESTING

Now it's time for testing. A **prototype** is tested to see if it does what it is supposed to do. Testing differs across the various fields of engineering. In electronic engineering, it might mean checking that electricity is flowing around a circuit properly. In mechanical engineering, it might mean operating a mechanism again and again to make sure that it works smoothly every time. In biochemical engineering, it could mean testing a drug over many months or even years. Engineers usually make a series of prototypes to iron out problems and make improvements.

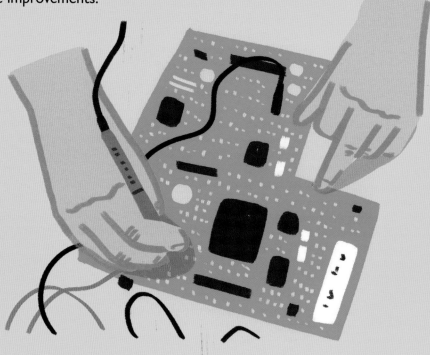

OUT OF CURIOSITY

Engineers sometimes deliberately test prototype machines until the machines fall to pieces, in order to see how long the machine will last. This is known as destructive testing.

✔ MAKING MODELS

In some fields of engineering, especially transportation, engineers build models to test. Sometimes these are full-scale models. In the case of a car, the model is placed in a wind tunnel, where air is blown over it to test its **aerodynamics** (the more smoothly the air flows over the car, the less fuel it will use). Engineers can then adjust the car's shape if necessary. Wind-tunnel tests are performed with model aircraft, and model ships are tested in huge tanks of water.

✘ WHEN THINGS GO WRONG

In engineering, things don't always go according to plan! **Prototype** machines can fail completely. In the case of spacecraft launch vehicles or aircraft, a test failure can mean that a prototype is destroyed. However, by examining wreckage and data recorded before the failure, engineers may find out what went wrong and make improvements to the design.

COMPUTER POWER

Computers are an important tool in the engineering design process. Engineers need three-dimensional models of the things—from skyscrapers to microchips—that they are designing. The models are used to print plans and diagrams of the objects on paper or prototypes on 3D printers.

COMPUTER-AIDED DESIGN

Building a model of an object on a computer is known as **computer-aided design** (CAD for short). With CAD software, an engineer can build objects, resize and rotate them, and copy and paste onto the objects, slowly building up parts to make a finished model. It also allows engineers to see how parts fit together. Textures can be applied to different parts to add realism. Engineers can view the model at any angle and any scale and make changes before building a real-life prototype. Moving parts of the machine, such as wheels and gears, can be animated in the model.

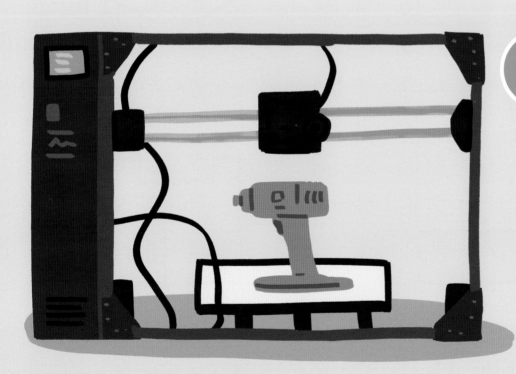

SIMULATING FORCES

A simulation uses software to calculate things such as the forces and movements that would happen in a machine or structure while it's in use. Civil engineers use simulations to find out the stresses (squashing and stretching forces) and strains (how much materials are squashed or stretched) on structures such as bridges. This is known as **structural analysis**. It shows where the greatest stresses and strains will be. Engineers can change the forces on a simulated structure (such as the weight of traffic on a bridge) to see how the structure reacts.

OUT OF CURIOSITY

Civil engineers have experimented with 3D printing for buildings. A giant 3D printer builds walls by adding layers of quick-setting concrete, one on top of the other.

3D PRINTING

Once an engineer has built a computer model of an object, a physical **prototype** can be made with a **3D printer**. All the parts of a machine can be printed to see if they fit together correctly. 3D printers can print complex shapes from many materials, including plastics, metals, and carbon-reinforced plastic, building the shapes layer by layer. 3D printing is also used to manufacture small numbers of objects.

COMMUNICATING IDEAS

Communicating is the final stage of the design process. Once prototyping and testing are complete, a gadget, machine, or structure is ready to be manufactured or built. Engineers then share the details of their designs to the people who will do this work.

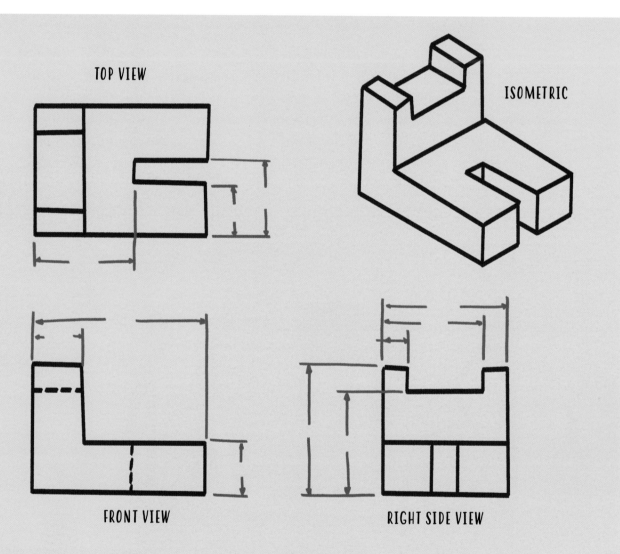

TOP VIEW

ISOMETRIC

FRONT VIEW

RIGHT SIDE VIEW

TECHNICAL DRAWINGS

A technical drawing shows the exact shape and size of an object or part of a machine. Most technical drawings show what an object looks like from different angles (from above, the front, and side), along with a 3D view (called an **isometric view**). Lines and arrows are dimensions—they show information about the size of the object, the depth of cuts, and diameter of holes. There might be hundreds of these drawings for all the parts of a complex machine. Along with the diagrams, engineers specify what materials parts need to be made from.

FOLLOWING PLANS

Some civil engineers design buildings and other structures, while others work on construction sites. The designers draw up detailed plans for the builders. The plans show all the information that the builders need—all the parts of a structure, materials they are made from, sizes and shapes, and how they fit together. There will be more drawings to show how water pipes, electricity cables, and other equipment fits in the building. For a major structure, such as a skyscraper, there could be hundreds of drawings for the builders to follow.

KEEPING THINGS WORKING

The story of a gadget, machine, or building is not over once manufacturing or building is complete. Things have to be serviced, or maintained, and fixed if they break down. Service or field engineers do these jobs. Engineers write maintenance manuals for service and field engineers to follow, which show all the parts of a machine and what parts need to be checked regularly.

CHAPTER 3

CIVIL ENGINEERING

Civil engineering is engineering on a giant scale.
Civil engineers build structures such as skyscrapers, bridges,
tunnels, roads, stadiums, and dams. Buildings create space for
living, for working, and for sports. Roads, bridges, and tunnels
help us travel from place to place.

In this chapter, we'll find out about concrete and steel,
the superstrong materials that civil engineers build with.
We'll find out what civil engineers do before they even pour
any concrete, and we'll discover the tricks civil engineers use
to make sure that buildings and bridges don't collapse.

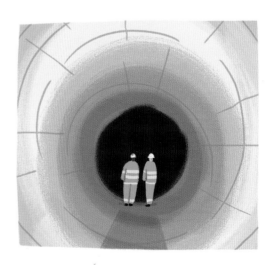

CONCRETE AND STEEL

Most civil engineering would be impossible without two materials: concrete and steel. These are used on their own for structures and foundations, but more importantly they are used in combination to make a superstrong material called reinforced concrete.

POURING CONCRETE

Concrete is a rock-hard material when it sets. It is made up of gravel, sand, cement, and water. Cement is like the glue that holds the gravel and sand together. When the ingredients are mixed, the water and cement react together and, over a few hours, become very hard. Concrete is extremely hard to crush. Engineers say that it has strong **compression**. Concrete is made into shapes by pouring it into casts while it's wet.

STEEL BEAMS

Steel is a mixture of iron and a little carbon. It's very difficult to stretch or squash—it's strong in **tension** and **compression**. Steel can be made into girders, rods, cables, and nuts and bolts. Girders for beams and columns are made from flat steel plates welded together. The most common shape has an I-shaped cross section. This is a strong shape that resists bending.

CONCRETE AND STEEL TOGETHER

Reinforced concrete is made from concrete with steel embedded in it. It combines the very high compressive strength of concrete with the very high **tensile strength** of steel, making a material that is stronger than either concrete or steel. Most concrete that you see in buildings, bridges, and other structures is reinforced concrete. A reinforced concrete beam is much stronger than a beam made just of concrete. To make a beam like this, steel bars are placed inside a cast and concrete is poured around them.

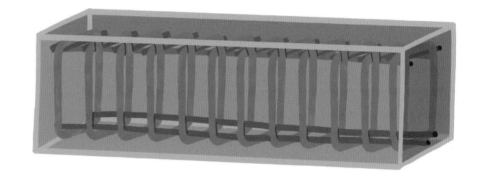

MORE MATERIALS

Concrete and steel are not the only materials used in civil engineering. Engineers make use of ceramics, glass, plastics, plus metals such as aluminum and copper. Ceramics are used for tiling and waterproofing, glass for walls and roofs, and plastics for cladding and insulation. Rubber is used for bridge-bearing plates—the pads that beams rest on, allowing the beams to move around and bend as heavy traffic passes over the bridge.

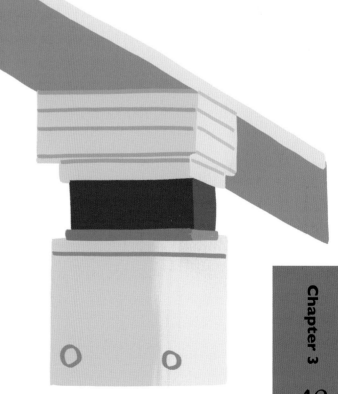

SHAPE AND STRUCTURE

Bridges, skyscrapers, stadiums, and other buildings are structures.
Their job is to resist forces (which engineers call loads), such as the weight
of people and furniture inside a skyscraper, or the weight of vehicles crossing
a bridge. Civil engineers make use of strong shapes such as domes, triangles,
and tubes in structures.

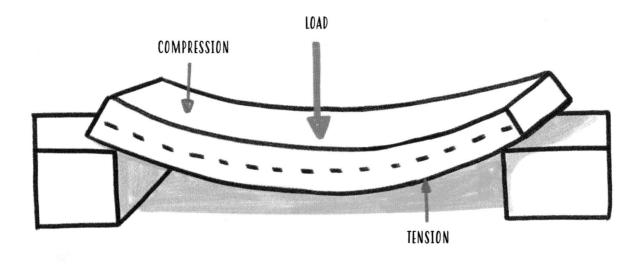

LOAD

COMPRESSION

TENSION

TENSION AND COMPRESSION

The loads on a beam try and bend it downward in the middle. Bending makes the
top of the beam get a little shorter and the bottom of the beam a little longer.
This squeezes the top of the beam, meaning that the material in the beam is in
compression, and stretches the bottom of the beam, meaning that the material
here is in **tension**. The longer the beam and the heavier the load, the stronger
the beam needs to be so that it doesn't bend too much.

OUT OF CURIOSITY

**Engineers have used nature as an inspiration many times in the history
of engineering. One example is the egg, which has dome-shaped ends
that can support a surprisingly large weight before the egg breaks.**

KEEPING SHAPE

The triangle is an important shape for civil engineers because of its strength. A simple rectangular frame (called an unbraced frame) is not very strong when pushed from the side, so it bends out of shape. This might happen to a building during strong winds. If a diagonal **brace** is added (to make a braced frame), a strong triangle is made. This means that the frame is much better at resisting the sideways push. Engineers also use triangles in structures called **trusses**, which are used for long bridge beams and roof supports.

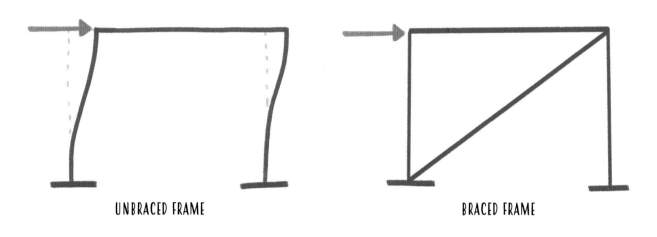

UNBRACED FRAME   BRACED FRAME

STRONG CURVES

Arches and domes are also very strong shapes. These shapes are used in bridges, tunnels, and in the roofs of buildings. Arches and domes are strong because the loads on them go around and down into the ground. This means the materials they are made from are only in **compression** and not in **tension**. Engineers have understood this for a very long time—most bridges were stone or iron arches until steel and concrete became available. A **geodesic** dome is a lightweight structure for making the walls and roof of a building. It's strong because of its dome shape and because the frame is made of triangles.

STRUCTURAL PARTS

The structure of a building or bridge directs the loads on it safely down to the ground. In a building, the loads on the floors are carried through the frame and foundations. Engineers design all the parts so they are strong enough to keep the building from collapsing.

FRAMES

All large buildings have frames that support their floors, walls, and roofs. A frame is made up of columns and beams, along with **bracing** to stabilize the frame. The edges of the floors, which are **reinforced concrete** slabs, sit on the beams. The thin outside walls hang on the beams or columns. A frame can be made of reinforced concrete, steel, or sometimes a combination of both. The bases of the columns sit on strong **foundations** to keep them from sinking into the ground.

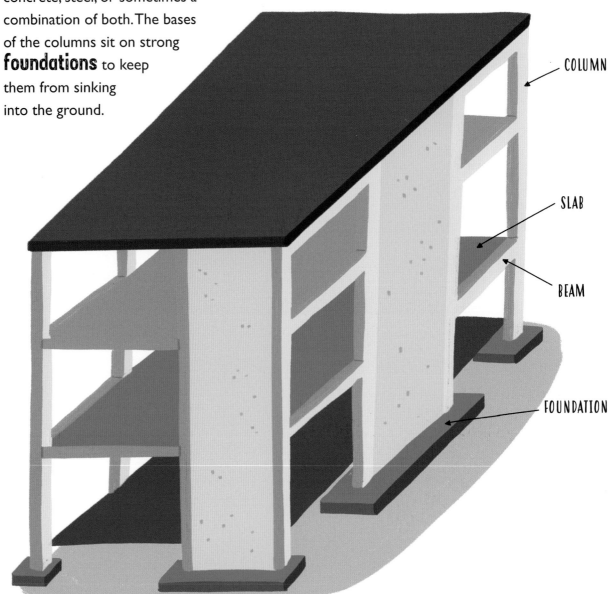

COLUMN

SLAB

BEAM

FOUNDATION

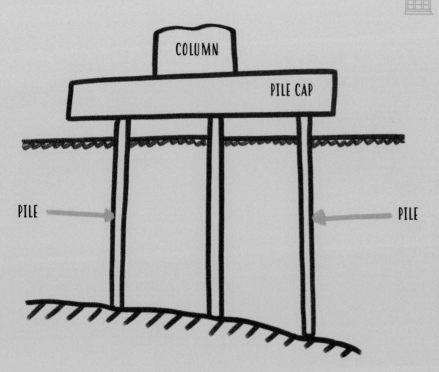

CONNECTING TO THE GROUND

All buildings need strong **foundations** to prevent them from sinking into the ground and to keep them stable. Engineers choose what kind of foundation to use depending on the type of soil or rock on the site of the building. A slab foundation is the simplest option. This is a wide concrete slab that sits on the ground and spreads out the weight of the building. A pile foundation is a long steel or concrete post that is driven into the ground. It grips the earth or reaches down to hard bedrock. Similar foundations are used for bridges and other structures.

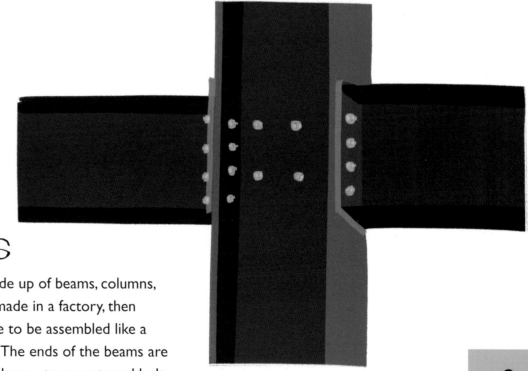

ASSEMBLING

A steel building frame is made up of beams, columns, and other parts. These are made in a factory, then delivered to the building site to be assembled like a giant kit to make the frame. The ends of the beams are bolted to the columns with large, strong nuts and bolts. The nuts and bolts are tightened to keep the joints from slipping. In a concrete frame, the joints are made by pouring concrete around reinforcing steel bars.

GROUND ENGINEERING

Engineers talk to geologists, who know about rocks and soils, to make sure that the ground is strong enough to support a new building. They may also need to move huge amounts of rock and soil, especially for building roads, rail lines, and dams.

WHAT'S BELOW?

Before engineers can design the foundations for a structure, they need to know what rocks are under the ground at the building site. There may be hard or soft rocks at the surface, or layers of soft rock over layers of hard rock. A **geological survey** is undertaken to discover what's there. Holes are drilled and samples of rock brought to the surface. These are analyzed by **geologists** to measure their strength.

EARTH MOVING

Engineers need to move earth to level the ground, perhaps before building a stadium or new houses, to create passages for roads or train lines to pass through, and to build up earth embankments for roads or trains to run along. Earth-moving equipment includes excavators to dig up earth, trucks to carry it around, plus scrapers and bulldozers to level the ground.

CLAY CORE

WATER

EARTH BANK

OUT OF CURIOSITY

The world's largest earth-filled dam is the Tarbela Dam in Pakistan, which was completed in 1976 to produce hydroelectric power. This massive structure is 143 m (469 ft) high and 2.7 km (1.7 mi) long.

EARTH STRUCTURES

Some civil engineering structures are made of earth and rock. The largest of these are earth dams and embankments. Like other engineering materials, different types of earth and rocks have different properties, so engineers use the materials for different jobs. A cross section of an earth dam (above) reveals a core made of clay, which is waterproof. Earth is compacted on top to make it firm.

 # ARTIFICIAL ISLANDS

Rocks are also used for building artificial islands at sea. The islands are built up by piling rocks on the seafloor to form a mound. Heavy rocks protect the island against rough seas. Artificial islands are used to create land for building on and where roads or train lines go from bridges to tunnels on sea crossings, such as this bridge-tunnel in China (left).

DESIGNING SKYSCRAPERS

Building skyscrapers is a huge challenge for engineers. The buildings are very heavy and often narrow, perhaps with a hundred floors or more. These need to resist strong winds. Towers, wind turbines, and oil rigs present similar difficulties.

FRAMEWORKS

Like any large building, a skyscraper needs a strong frame to support its floors and walls. In most skyscrapers, the frame is hidden behind the walls, but sometimes it is placed on the outside as an architectural feature, as with the Morpheus Hotel in Macau, China (above). Many skyscrapers have a central core of **reinforced concrete** that provides a strong spine. Elevators and other services are inside the core. A steel frame surrounds the core to support the floors.

ARCHITECTS' DESIGNS

Architects design the overall look of a skyscraper. They start with a brief from the client. The brief says what the building will be used for, how many floors it will need, and where it's going to be built. The architect starts by sketching ideas for the new skyscraper. Once a final design has been agreed, engineers figure out exactly how the structure will carry the loads, then design all the building's parts and how they will fit together.

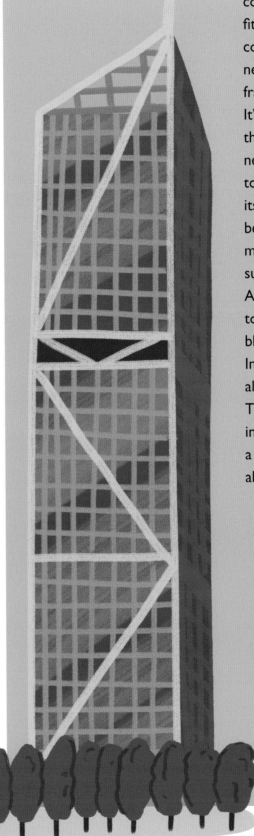

RESISTING FORCES

It's not just a building's contents—people, furniture, fittings such as bathrooms, computers, and so on—that need to be held up by its frame and foundations. It's also the huge weight of the building itself. Engineers need to design a building to be strong enough to do its job—but no stronger because this would add more weight in materials such as steel and concrete. A skyscraper must be able to resist the force of wind blowing against its sides. In some countries, it must also resist earthquakes. The Fremont Tower (left) in San Francisco, USA, has a special frame that can absorb movement.

REACHING THE HEIGHTS

Once a skyscraper has been designed, construction can begin. Building a skyscraper is a very complicated job, often made more complicated when the building site is in a busy city. A team of engineers organizes the building process.

BUILDING STAGES

The process of building a skyscraper begins with clearing the site and putting down the **foundations**. Skyscrapers always have deep pile foundations because of the immense weight of the building. The central core is next. As this rises upward, the frame for each floor is built around it. After this, the floors are added one by one, and the **curtain walls** are placed on the outside of the frame. Indoor work on the lower floors starts before the concrete core reaches its full height. Construction cranes are not tall enough to reach so high from the ground, so they are attached to the core and frame.

CONCRETE CORES

Many skyscrapers have a concrete core—a superstrong **reinforced concrete** tube that runs up the middle of the building. A core is built by pouring concrete into a cast that contains steel reinforcing bars and allowing the concrete to set. This creates a new section of the core. Then the cast is moved up, and another section formed in the same way. Sometimes the cast moves upward continuously. Concrete is poured into the top, and it sets by the time it comes out of the bottom. This is called **slip forming**.

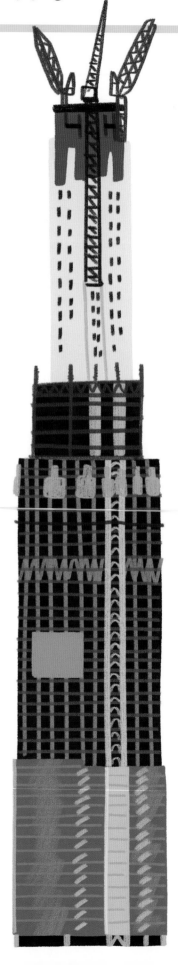

 BUILDING AT SEA

Super-tall structures at sea include offshore wind farms, oil platforms that sit on the seabed, and towers that support bridges across wide areas of sea. The mast of a wind turbine is a steel tube that holds up the turbine itself and resists bending. The legs of an oil platform are towers made of steel frameworks or concrete tubes. The parts of these structures are made on land and transported to sea for assembly. Special machinery, such as gigantic floating cranes, are used to carry and position the parts.

BUILDING BRIDGES

Bridges carry vehicles, trains, and pedestrians over rivers, deep valleys, roads, and rail lines. Super-long or high bridges, especially over water, are challenging structures for engineers to design and construct.

TYPES OF BRIDGES

The main types of bridges are the arch, beam, cantilever, cable-stayed, and suspension bridge. The structure of each bridge supports weight in a different way. The downward force from the traffic crossing the bridge (called the load) is carried to the ground by a different route.

ARCH BRIDGE

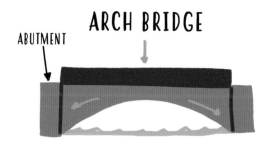

- The force of the load tries to squash the arch.
- The ends of the arch push sideways into the heavy abutments.

BEAM BRIDGE

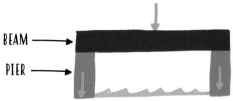

- The force of the load tries to bend the beam.
- The beam presses down on the piers.

CANTILEVER

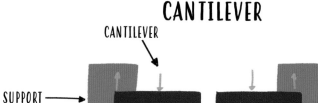

- The force of the load tries to bend the cantilevers.
- Each cantilever pulls down and pushes up on its support.

CABLE STAYED

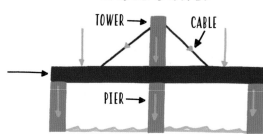

- The force of the load pushes down on the deck.
- The deck pulls on the cables, and the cables pull down and sideways on the tower.
- The deck and tower push down on the piers.

SUSPENSION

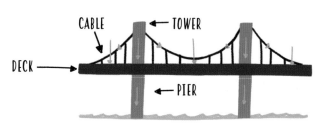

- The force of the load pushes down on the deck.
- The deck pulls on the cables, and the cables pull down and sideways on the towers.
- The towers push down on the piers.

ENGINEERING DECISIONS

Engineers take many different factors into account when they design a new bridge. What traffic will cross the bridge? Does the bridge cross land or water? What soils and rocks are under the site of the bridge? How far does the bridge need to stretch without supports? Is it very windy at the site? When these questions are answered, they can decide what type of bridge to use and design its parts to make it strong enough. A bridge must support the weight of the things that travel over it and the weight of the steel, concrete, and other materials that it's made from.

OUT OF CURIOSITY

The world's longest sea bridge is the Hong Kong–Zhuhai–Macau bridge. It opened in 2018 to link three cities in China across a wide bay. Engineers built the enormous towers on land and transported and lifted them into position with huge barges and floating cranes.

 # BUILDING A BRIDGE

Building starts with the **foundations** for the bridge's piers, towers, and other supports. If the supports are going to stand in water, a circular dam called a **cofferdam** is built and the water pumped out, so that the foundations can be built. Once the bridge's supports are in place, the deck can be positioned.

RADICAL FOOTBRIDGES

In recent years, engineers have designed and built footbridges with amazing shapes, some even with glass walkways. These bridges have more complicated structures than traditional bridges and would not be possible to design without computers that analyze the forces on the different parts of the structure.

TUNNEL ENGINEERING

Digging tunnels is a very challenging civil engineering job that requires expert knowledge and special machinery. Modern tunnels are built either by blasting away rock with explosives or by cutting away rock with machinery. Long tunnels are dug with tunnel-boring machines.

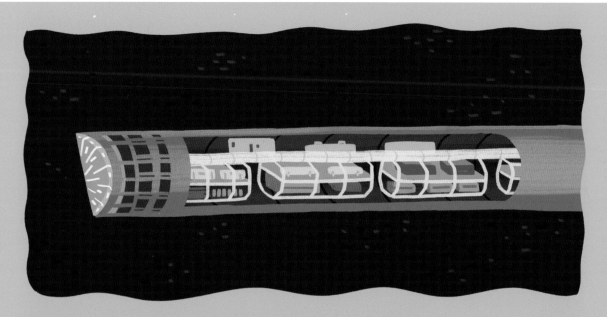

TUNNEL-BORING MACHINES

A tunnel-boring machine (TBM for short) is like a giant drill that eats its way through solid rock. At the front of a TBM is a rotating cutting head full of sharp teeth that cut away the rock. **Hydraulic** rams push the cutting head forward. Broken rock (called **spoil**) is carried away by conveyor belts behind the cutting head. Sections of tunnel lining are put into place to support the walls and roof of the tunnel.

BREAKING THROUGH

Before a tunnel is started, engineers carefully plan its route through the rock below ground. It might need to stay at a certain depth below a river, or avoid existing tunnels or weak rock that might collapse. A TBM is guided by lasers, turning gently up, down, left, or right, to make sure it follows the correct route and emerges in the right place. Very long tunnels are often drilled from both ends, so accurate guidance is vital to ensure that the two tunnels meet each other underground.

SPECIAL DIGGERS

It's usually too expensive to use a tunnel-boring machine for short sections of tunnel. Instead, the digging is done by excavators that are fitted with rotating cutters that nibble away at the rock. Loaders and trucks scoop up and carry away the **spoil**. A smooth tunnel lining is made by spraying concrete onto the walls and roof.

SUBMERGED TUNNELS

Not all underwater tunnels are built by digging through the ground under a river or seabed. Some are submerged-tube tunnels. In shallow water, giant steel or concrete tubes are lowered into the water and connected to create a tunnel. The tubes are covered with rocks for protection and to prevent them from floating to the surface.

63

CITY ENGINEERING

Civil engineers help keep towns and cities running. They design and operate highways and other transportation systems to enable cars, trains, and people to move around efficiently. They also build and maintain vital services, such as water supplies and sanitation systems.

KEEPING VEHICLES RUNNING

Most big cities suffer with traffic congestion. It's up to engineers to solve these problems by designing new highway systems that keep the traffic moving—getting it across and in and out of a city. That means building new roads, intersections, and complex interchanges where traffic can switch from one road to another without stopping. This often involves designing and building bridges and tunnels to allow roads to cross each other.

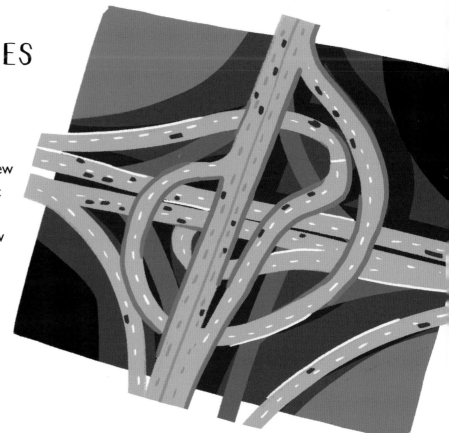

MASS TRANSIT

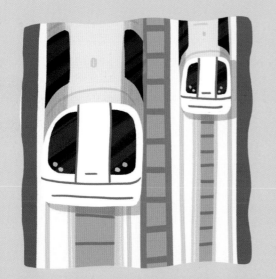

Mass transit means moving large numbers of people in, out, and around cities quickly and efficiently. It is normally some type of rail system, which might be surface trains, subway trains, elevated trains, or streetcars (also called trams). Building a new mass-transportation system can mean digging tunnels under roads or building structures to keep trains high above the streets—never easy in a busy city. New ideas for mass transit include small, driverless pods, each carrying several passengers, such as the system in use between terminals at London Heathrow Airport, UK.

DRAINAGE

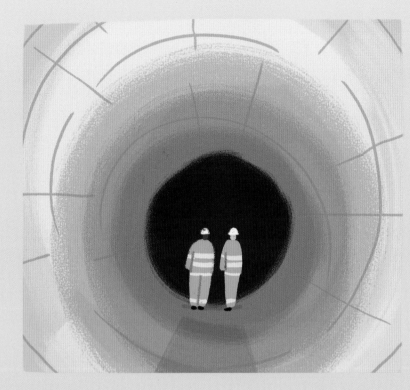

Homes, restaurants, and factories in cities create huge amounts of wastewater, sewage (waste from toilets), and drainage water from the streets. Hidden under the streets are complex systems of sewers and pipes that take away this water—the dirty water and sewage to be cleaned and the drainage into rivers or the sea. In the biggest cities, these pipes can be vast tunnels. Engineers also design and build water-supply systems that bring clean water into cities.

FLOOD PROTECTION

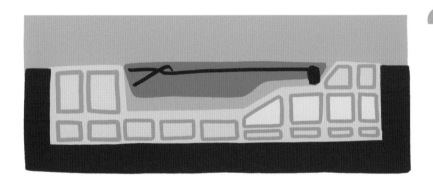

Towns and cities on coasts or next to major rivers are always at risk from floods. These risks are increasing as global warming brings rising sea levels and more extreme weather. Engineers design and build flood-protection schemes to reduce the risk. Flood barriers, such as the ones in Venice, Italy (left), rise when a city is threatened by very high tides. Here, water is pumped out of the gates to make them float and block the water.

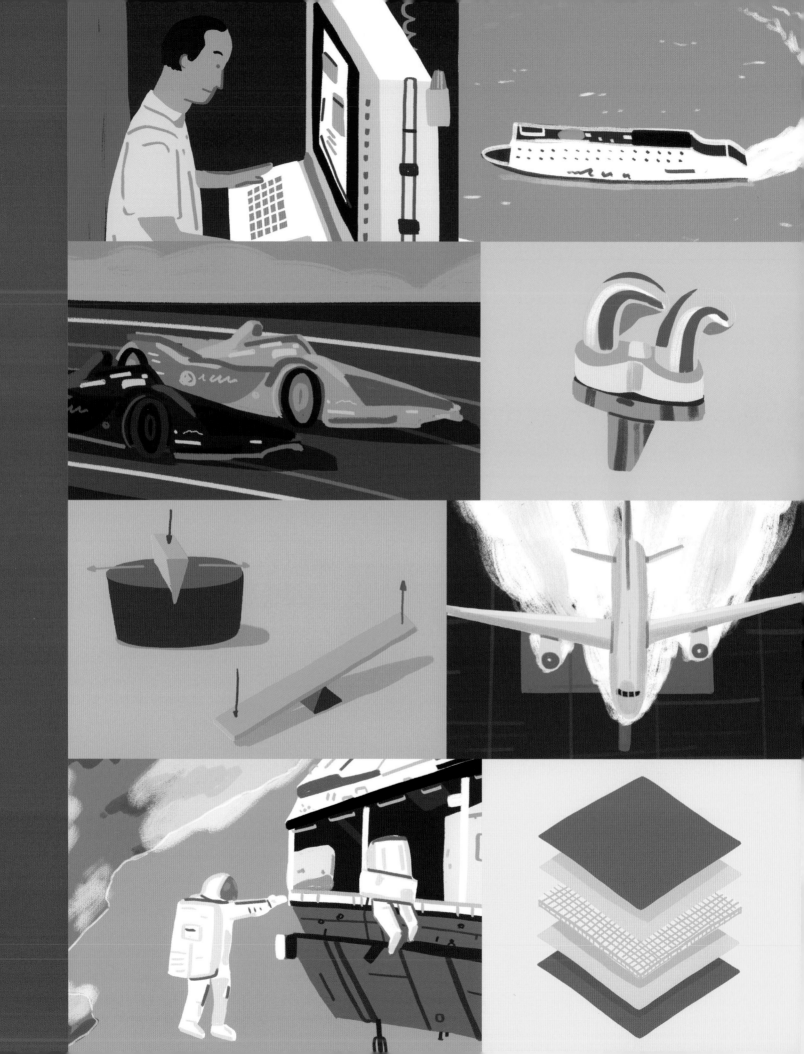

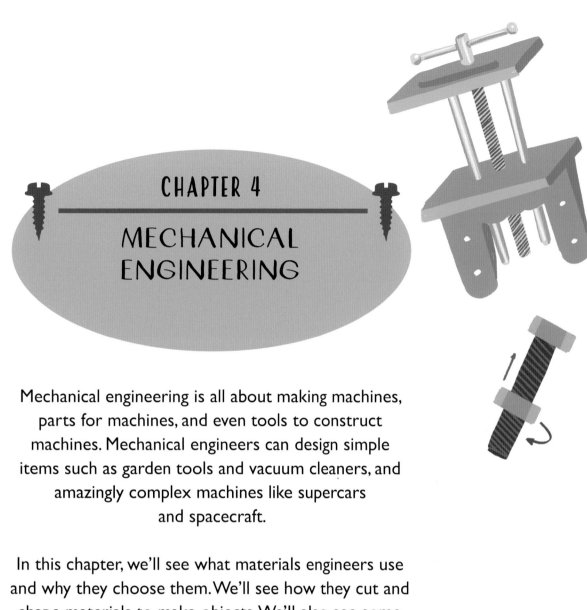

CHAPTER 4

MECHANICAL ENGINEERING

Mechanical engineering is all about making machines, parts for machines, and even tools to construct machines. Mechanical engineers can design simple items such as garden tools and vacuum cleaners, and amazingly complex machines like supercars and spacecraft.

In this chapter, we'll see what materials engineers use and why they choose them. We'll see how they cut and shape materials to make objects. We'll also see some of the mechanisms that engineers put inside machines and how they apply all these skills to car, plane, ship, and spacecraft production.

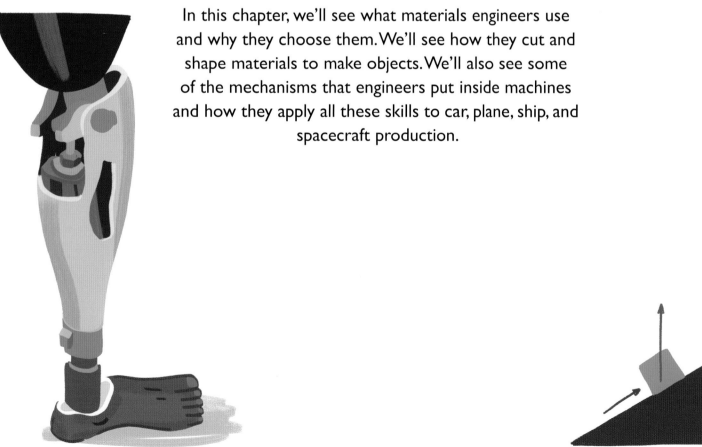

⦗⦘ MATERIALS ⦗⦘

Mechanical engineers work with a huge variety of materials, including metals, plastics, and ceramics. Engineers select materials for a job by considering the medium's density, hardness, ductility, malleability, stretchiness, and chemical properties.

⦗⦘ METALS AND ALLOYS

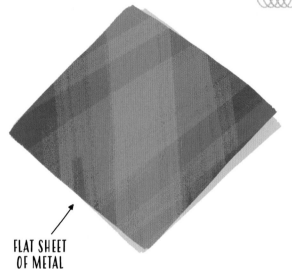

FLAT SHEET
OF METAL

Engineers make things from iron, steel (which is mostly iron), aluminum, titanium, copper, brass, and many other metals. Most metals are strong and hard but also **malleable** and **ductile**, which means that they can be hammered and bent into shape. Ductility allows a sheet of metal to be pressed into a three-dimensional shape, such as a bowl. It also allows metals to be drawn (pulled) into thin wires. **Alloys** are made by mixing metals to get the best properties from both metals. For example, stainless steel, which doesn't rust, is made by adding chromium to steel.

FORCE PUSHING DOWN

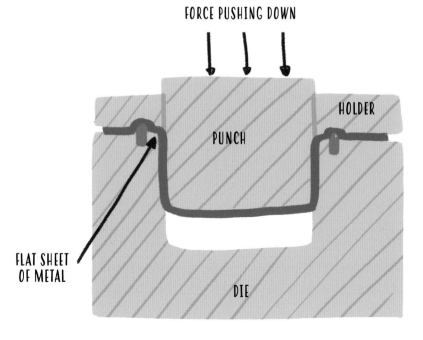

HOLDER

PUNCH

FLAT SHEET
OF METAL

DIE

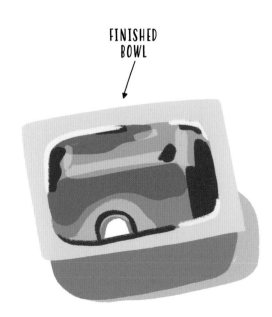

FINISHED
BOWL

STRETCHING AND SQUASHING

Some materials are **elastic**, which is a useful property for engineers. When you stretch, squash, or bend a piece of an elastic material then let go, it returns to its original shape. Rubber is a very elastic material, so it's used in vehicle suspensions. Some metals are also elastic—they are used to make objects such as springs. Composite materials can be elastic, too—a pole-vault pole is made from very elastic glass-reinforced plastic (see page 70). Engineers make sure that elastic materials are not stretched too much since they can change shape permanently or break.

CERAMICS

Pottery and glass are examples of ceramics. Ceramics are hard and brittle (which means that they snap instead of stretch), so they are not normally used for parts of machines, but they have high melting points and are good **insulators** (so heat can't flow through them well). They are also good electrical insulators, which means that electricity can't flow through them. Ceramic insulators hold up power lines to keep the electricity from flowing into the pylons.

COMPOSITES

A composite material is made from two or more materials combined. Composite materials, such as glass-reinforced plastic and carbon-reinforced plastic, are useful because they have different properties compared to the materials they are made from. Engineers use composites because they are normally strong and lightweight.

GLASS

PLASTIC

GLASS-REINFORCED PLASTIC

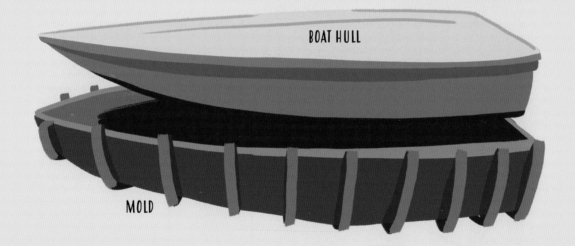

BOAT HULL

MOLD

GLASS-REINFORCED PLASTIC

Glass and plastic go together to make glass-reinforced plastic (GRP). The glass is a thin mat made of very fine strands. The plastic is resin that is runny when made and sets hard. To make GRP, the plastic resin is poured or brushed over the glass mat in a cast. GRP is stronger than glass or plastic, lightweight, durable, and easy to shape. Engineers use it to make anything from boat hulls to wind turbine blades.

CARBON COMPOSITES

Carbon-reinforced plastic is a composite material similar to glass-reinforced plastic. It's made from filaments of carbon contained in plastic resin. The filaments are made from pure carbon and are thinner than a human hair. They are spun into yarn and then woven into mats. The composite material is made by pouring or brushing resin over the carbon mat. Engineers use carbon-reinforced plastic when they need a very light but strong material—for anything from kayak paddles and crash helmets to aircraft wings.

OUT OF CURIOSITY

A carbon fiber is five times stronger than steel, but it is just half the weight. By reducing the overall weight of a structure, it can reduce costs.

LAMINATES

A **laminate** is a composite material made from flat sheets of different materials stacked on top of each other and glued together. Wood-patterned floors, countertops, and plywood are all laminate materials. Laminates can take the place of other materials but be stronger and lighter. Many laminates have three layers—a central honeycomb layer and two skins glued to the top and bottom. Cardboard is an everyday example. Similar laminates, made from aluminum or plastics, are used to make strong panels for doors, floors, and walls in vehicles and aircraft wings.

SHAPING TOOLS

Engineers create parts for machines by shaping materials. They cut, drill, mill, press, turn, and cast materials using a variety of machine tools. They use computer-controlled machinery to craft parts with great accuracy.

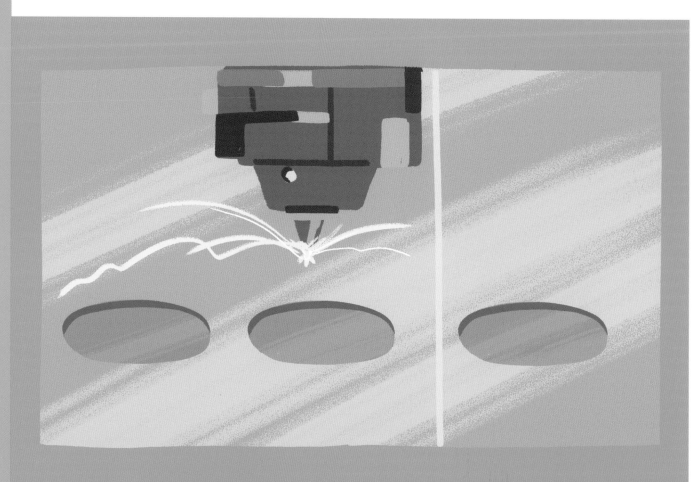

CUTTING

Cutting removes unwanted pieces of material by chopping them off. A saw is the simplest cutting machine for hard materials such as wood, plastic, and metal. Machine tools for sawing include disk saws (which have a cutting disk) and band saws (which have a cutting blade in the form of a continuous loop). A laser cutting machine cuts complex shapes from sheet materials. It has a powerful laser that heats and melts the material almost instantly as it cuts.

DRILLING AND MILLING

Drilling and milling machines cut away material with a spinning blade called a **bit**. A drilling machine makes holes in materials by pushing a spinning drill bit through the material. Holes are normally made for joining parts together with nuts and bolts. A milling machine cuts away material with a spinning bit that cuts sideways. It can cut complex shapes from a block of material.

AUTOMATIC MACHINES

Machine tools, such as milling machines, can be operated manually, but automated machines are used for mass production since they can make many pieces exactly the same much more quickly than a human operator can. The cuts that are needed to make a shape are programmed into the machine, and it repeats these moves very accurately. Computer-controlled machines like this are known as CNC (computer numerical control) machines.

CASTING

Casting is another way of shaping materials. Casting can only be used with materials that can be melted, such as metals and glass, or materials that start as liquids and then set hard, such as plastic resins. The liquid material is poured into the cast, allowed to cool or set, then the cast is broken open to remove the part. Parts from truck engine blocks to plastic bottles are made by casting.

SIMPLE MACHINES

A mechanism is a system of parts in a machine that work together.
It can be as simple as a pair of scissors or as complicated as
a vehicle gearbox. Engineers often use basic mechanisms called simple machines
as building blocks for more complex mechanisms.

WEDGE   SCREW   INCLINED PLANE

SIX SIMPLE MACHINES

There are six simple machines. These are the lever, pulley, **wedge**, inclined **plane**, screw thread, and wheel and **axle**. These machines can be used to increase or decrease a force, make things move faster or slower, or fix things in position. The lever is a very common mechanism. You'll find it in simple tools such as pliers (where it increases force) and tweezers (where it decreases force), and as part of complex machines, such as aircraft undercarriages. The wheel and axle is vital in gearboxes used in computer printers, cars, and aircraft engines.

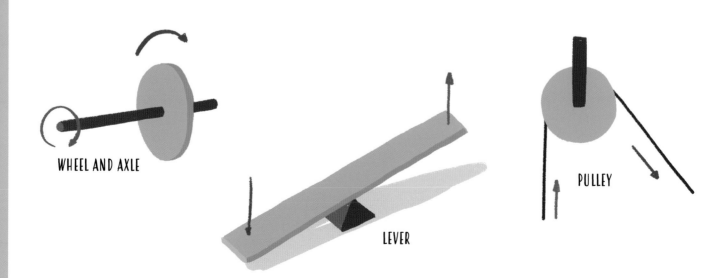

WHEEL AND AXLE   LEVER   PULLEY

PULLEYS AT WORK

The pulley is one of the six simple machines. It's most often seen on building-site cranes, where it increases the pulling force generated by a motor, so that the crane can lift heavy objects. You will find pulleys in garden tools and on sailboats, too. A pulley system is made up of two pulley blocks containing pulley wheels, with a rope going from block to block around the pulley wheels. The more times the rope goes between the pulley blocks, the more the pulley system can increase a force.

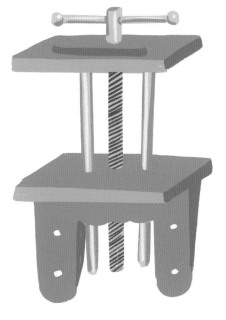

SCREWS AT WORK

The screw thread is also a simple machine, and it's vital in mechanical engineering. Screws and nuts and bolts have a screw thread. With a nut and bolt, one turn of the nut moves the nut the length of one groove on the bolt. This allows the nut and bolt to squeeze two parts of a machine tightly together using a small amount of effort with a spanner. The screw thread on a vise does a similar job: a gentle push on the handle forces the jaws tightly together to hold an object securely in place.

AUTOMOTIVE ENGINEERING

Automotive engineering is the engineering of cars, trucks, motorcycles, and other vehicles. Automotive engineers design and build new models. They normally focus on one part of a vehicle, such as the body, the engine, or the suspension. They also do research and development into new technologies, for instance electric cars.

🚗 NEW DESIGNS

When a car manufacturing company wants to build a new car, engineers and designers work together to brainstorm ideas. They decide what function the car will have—it might be a family car, a sports car, or an off-road car. Designers work on the overall shape of the vehicle while engineers figure out the car's structure, and they design the thousands of parts the car needs, from the large body panels to the smallest nuts and bolts.

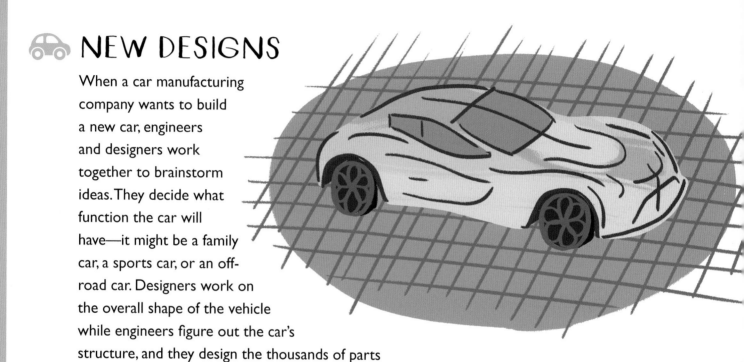

🚗 CRASH TESTING

Safety is very important in automotive engineering. Cars are designed to keep drivers and passengers as safe as possible if the car is involved in an accident. Safety features include seat restraints, air bags, and crush zones. All new models of cars must pass a series of safety tests before they go into mass production. These include tests where the car is deliberately crashed into solid metal blocks to make sure that the crush zones absorb the impact.

PRODUCTION LINES

Cars and other vehicles are assembled on a production line. Production starts with pressing and painting the body panels and assembling them to make the car's body shell. All the other parts are added as the car moves down the line. Car assembly lines are amazing pieces of engineering themselves with a lot of automation, including robots that paint and weld.

NEW TECHNOLOGIES

Auto engineering includes research and development—this means creating new technologies for vehicles. Many new technologies that we see on production cars (cars that we can buy), such as traction control, are first developed for race cars. In the world of car racing, engineers are constantly experimenting to gain hundredths of seconds over their rivals.

AERONAUTICAL ENGINEERING

Aeronautical engineering is all about designing and building aircraft. This can be anything from tiny drones to giant passenger airliners—some of the most complex machines engineers have ever built. Aeronautical engineers need to understand how aircraft fly—the science of aerodynamics.

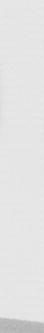

AIRCRAFT MATERIALS

Aeronautical engineers need materials that are strong but lightweight. Aluminum alloys are used widely in aircraft fuselages and wings, and often in the form of **laminates,** as are composites such as carbon-reinforced plastics. The fan blades at the front of engines move at extremely high speeds. They are made by casting titanium alloys or composites.

OUT OF CURIOSITY

Inside the engine, temperatures can reach more than 1,000° C (1,832° F). The turbine blades are made from nickel alloys, which have very high melting points. They are coated in ceramics to help keep them cool.

SAFETY TESTING

All new aircraft are put through intensive testing programs to make sure they are safe to fly with passengers. During test flights, engineers are on board to monitor systems such as fuel tanks and flight controls. Landing gear is raised and lowered hundreds of times. Aircraft also do **aquaplane** tests to make sure they won't skid when they land on flooded runways. Safety is vital in aircraft, so engineers design in "redundancy," so that if something fails, there's always a backup. Aircraft accidents are rare, but if they do happen, specialist engineers investigate to figure out what went wrong. If necessary, modifications are made to other aircraft.

DESTRUCTIVE TESTING

New types of jet engines are tested in the same way as other machines. A prototype is made and tested to make sure that it operates as planned. Does it generate as much power as it should? Does it overheat? How much fuel does it use? An object flying into an engine can make a fan blade fail. Engineers must make sure that, even if a fan blade is destroyed and the inside of the engine breaks up, nothing flies out of the engine casing that could damage the rest of the aircraft. So, a destructive test is conducted by deliberately breaking off a fan blade with the engine running at full power.

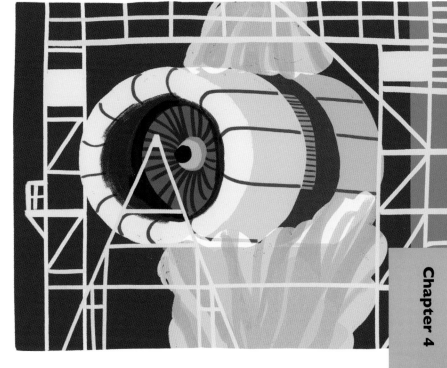

AEROSPACE ENGINEERING

The engineering skills of aeronautical engineering are also used to design and build spacecraft and the rockets that launch the spacecraft into orbit. That's why aeronautical engineering and space engineering are bundled together and called aerospace engineering.

SPACECRAFT CONSTRUCTION

Space is not a kind place for machinery. Spacecraft must cope with extreme temperatures, high levels of radiation, and huge forces during the launch and return to Earth. A crewed spacecraft (with astronauts) must also keep its crew safe in space and protected from roasting during Earth re-entry. Engineers must design systems for navigating in space, for steering, for life support, and for docking with other craft. Just as challenging is engineering robot space probes that travel far throughout the solar system to other planets and moons. Their systems must be tested again and again to make sure they will work years after launch and far away from Earth.

ENGINE TESTING

Launch vehicles are powered by super-powerful rocket engines. Launch vehicles can have several main engines plus smaller boosters. They must be engineered to withstand the huge forces and extreme temperatures they create. New engines undergo tests to make sure they create enough **thrust**. Launch vehicles also need fuel systems to feed the engines, guidance systems to steer them into orbit around Earth, and systems to jettison booster rockets and release spacecraft after launch. And everything must work at speeds up to 11 km (6.8 mi) per second—the speed needed to get into Earth orbit.

ASTRONAUT ENGINEERS

Spacecraft and launch vehicles are built by engineers down on the ground. But there's plenty of engineering to be done in space, especially on the International Space Station (ISS), and many astronauts are also expert engineers. The ISS was built in space by astronauts from parts that were launched from Earth. Things sometimes break down in space, and astronauts occasionally need to go on spacewalks to fix parts of the ISS.

MARINE ENGINEERING

Marine engineers design and build ships, boats, oil platforms, and other structures at sea. They also repair and maintain ships. The sea is a harsh environment where conditions can be rough, and salt water is corrosive, so ships must be engineered to withstand these conditions. Most large ships have an on-board engineer, too.

THINKING BIG

Building a ship is engineering on a huge scale. The largest cargo ships and cruise ships are as long as streets. A ship's hull is a structure that must resist twisting and bending as large waves pass under it. It's normally made up of boxlike steel sections that divide the ship into watertight compartments. Huge engines drive massive propellers, with blades curved for efficiency. They are made from metal alloys that resist **corrosion**.

SEA TRIALS

All ships are tested to make sure that they perform as they were designed to. These tests are called sea trials. Engineers are on board to monitor the maximum speed, how the ship slows down when engines are reversed, and how the ship tilts in tight turns. They also monitor the engines and check that the propellers are working smoothly without causing vibrations.

ON-BOARD ENGINEERS

Ship's engineers look after the engines, steering equipment, and electrical and navigation systems. The operation of all the on-board machinery is controlled and monitored electronically from a control room. Ship's engineers also carry out minor repairs at sea.

OIL PLATFORMS

Oil platforms are another example of engineering on a giant scale. These structures are used to drill into the seabed to search for oil or to bring oil to the surface. They are huge structures as tall as skyscrapers. Some float on the water, anchored in place, while others stand on the seabed on long legs. Their structures are engineered to withstand strong winds and large waves. The engineering task requires special ships to transport oil platforms to where they are needed.

BIOMEDICAL ENGINEERING

Biomedical engineers combine their mechanical engineering skills (and electronic engineering skills) with medical knowledge to create artificial limbs, artificial joints, and sometimes artificial organs. They help people who have lost limbs or whose joints are damaged or worn out.

 ## HI-TECH LEGS

An artificial leg or arm is called a **prosthetic** limb. Modern prosthetics are complex pieces of engineering. A prosthetic leg (right) is made for a person who has lost their leg above the knee. It has an articulated knee joint that swings back and forth in a natural way, allowing the person to walk. Motion sensors detect how fast the person swings their leg, and this data is fed to a small computer that controls how fast the knee joint moves. This is known as a "microprocessor knee." The socket at the top is made from carbon-reinforced plastic for lightness.

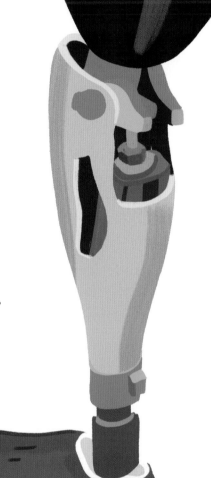

OUT OF CURIOSITY

Biomedical engineers make prosthetic lower legs for para athletes. These lightweight prosthetics are designed to be springy to replicate the feeling of a lower leg with a sports shoe on the foot.

BIONICS

Engineers are developing prosthetic limbs that are powered by on-board electric motors and controlled by the wearer. The joints mimic the movements of real arm and leg joints, and hands that close to grip objects. These prosthetics are often called **bionic** limbs. In an arm, electronics detect tiny electrical nerve signals that control the muscles in the upper arm. Electronics interpret the signals and control the motors that move the joints and fingers. It's still very difficult to make a bionic arm work exactly like a human arm, even for simple actions such as scratching your head.

REPLACEMENT JOINTS

Biomedical engineers also design and make replacement joints for people whose joints have worn out or been damaged by disease. Replacement hip and knee joints are most common. The parts of a replacement joint that replace worn bone are made from metals or alloys such as titanium, stainless steel, and cobalt-chromium. These are strong and light. Ceramics and tough plastics are placed between the metal parts to allow the joint to rotate smoothly.

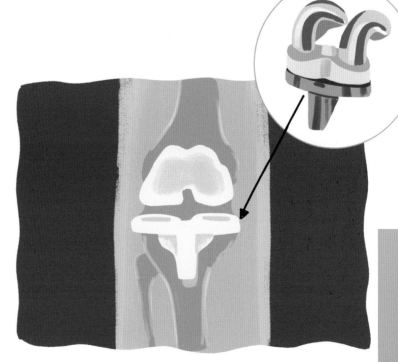

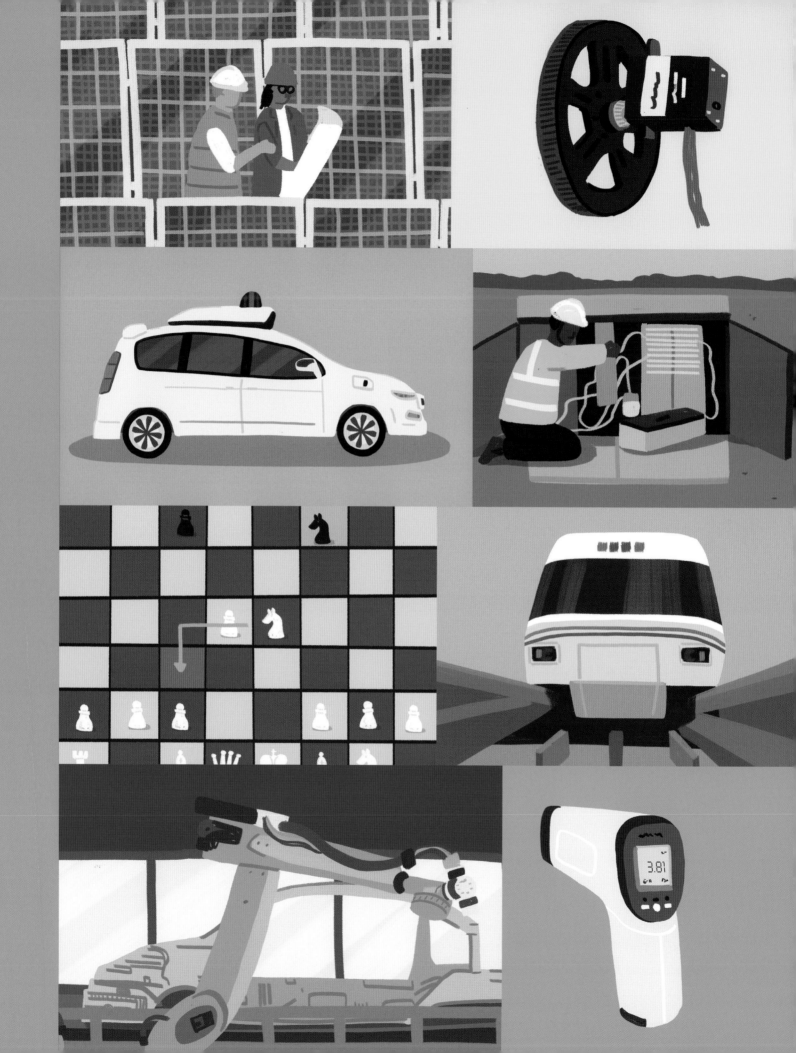

CHAPTER 5

ENGINEERING WITH ELECTRICITY

We rely on electricity and electronics every day. We need electricity to power our lights, heating, air conditioning, kitchen appliances, and vehicles to get us around. We rely on the electronics that make our phones, computers, and games consoles work, and the electronics that run the internet. We can thank electrical engineers and electronic engineers for all these things.

In this chapter we'll see how electrical and electronic engineers control electricity, making it work for us, how they build the microscopic circuits in microchips, and use their skills in communication systems, transport, and medicine.

DESIGNING CIRCUITS

Electrical and electronic engineers design, build, and test electric and electronic circuits, from those in a simple lamp to the complex circuits needed in electronic gadgets. Electrical and electronic specialists start by understanding what an electronics circuit is needed for.

 ## COMPONENTS

Circuits are paths for electric currents to flow through. They may include components such as batteries, **resistors, capacitors, transistors,** and **microchips.** Each component in a circuit has a job to do. A battery pushes electric current around a circuit, a resistor slows down the flow of current, a capacitor stores charge, and a transistor works like a switch. By connecting different components with metal wires or tracks, engineers can plan circuits for different jobs.

TRANSMISSION LINES

A complex grid of transmission lines carries electricity from power plants to electricity distribution stations in towns and cities. From there, the electricity flows along cables to homes, factories, offices, stores, and rail lines. Electrical engineers build, maintain, and repair these transmission lines. They also monitor and control where the flow of electricity from power plants goes to in towns and cities.

ELECTRICAL TRANSPORTATION

Electrical engineers also work on systems for electrically powered transportation such as streetcars, trams, and trains, including power supplies and overhead cables. These systems control the strong currents that power the electric motors in the trains. More electrical equipment is needed in the trains themselves. Magnetic levitation (**maglev**) tracks need complex electrical systems, too, to operate the powerful electromagnets that make the trains run.

? OUT OF CURIOSITY

Experimental maglev trains make use of superconducting magnets. These are electromagnets with electric coils made of superconductors—materials that have almost no resistance to electricity.

All modern electronic gadgets contain microchips (also called integrated circuits). Microchips are made up of miniaturized electronic components (transistors, resistors, and capacitors), all built into a single chip of silicon.

MICROSCOPIC SCALE

Making microchips is engineering on an extremely tiny scale. The components are so small that they can only be seen with a microscope. The smallest measure a few nanometers across—that's just a few millionths of a centimeter. The chips are made from a material called **silicon**, which is found in sand. Silicon can be treated to make it into a **conductor,** an **insulator,** or a **semiconductor**—a material that can switch between being a conductor and an insulator.

MICROCHIP DESIGN

The position of each component and the tracks that connect them is calculated using software. Then a prototype chip is built. A chip starts as a single piece of **silicon**, then layers of different types of silicon are added to build up the components and connections. There can be up to a hundred layers on a single chip.

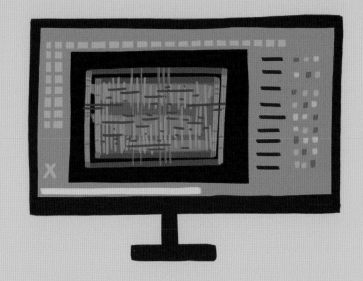

ENGINEERING WITH LIGHT

Every layer of the chip is coated with photosensitive material called **photoresist**. The chip is put into a **photolithography** machine, which focuses a picture of the next layer onto the silicon using a lens. This creates the pattern of the layer in the resist. The chip is baked, then the remaining resist is washed away. Then, chemicals are used to treat the **silicon** that's not covered by the resist, creating the new layer. This process is repeated again and again to build up the numerous layers.

OUT OF CURIOSITY

The main processing chip in a modern laptop computer contains between two and three billion transistors.

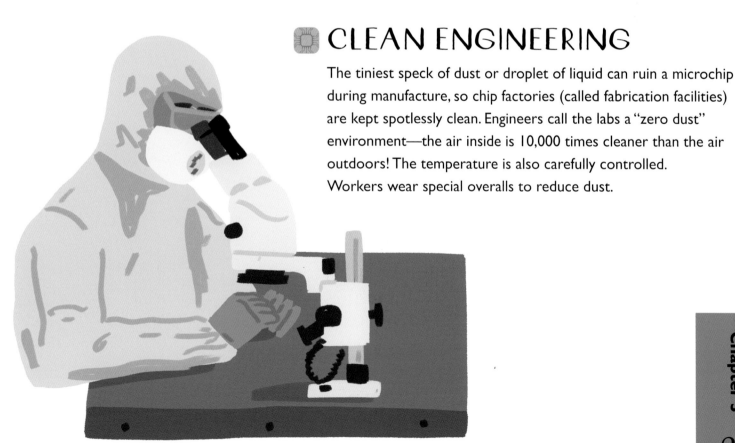

CLEAN ENGINEERING

The tiniest speck of dust or droplet of liquid can ruin a microchip during manufacture, so chip factories (called fabrication facilities) are kept spotlessly clean. Engineers call the labs a "zero dust" environment—the air inside is 10,000 times cleaner than the air outdoors! The temperature is also carefully controlled. Workers wear special overalls to reduce dust.

TELECOMMUNICATIONS

Electrical engineers build and maintain communication systems including phone networks, the Internet, television, and cable networks. Engineers work on data centers, underground and undersea cables, satellites, and Wi-Fi networks.

DATA CENTERS

Data centers are connected to the Internet. They store data that Internet users can access online, such as photographs in cloud storage, data for websites, and emails. They include storage systems (where the data is held), servers that send out information to Internet users, power supplies to keep everything running, backup power supplies, and cooling systems.

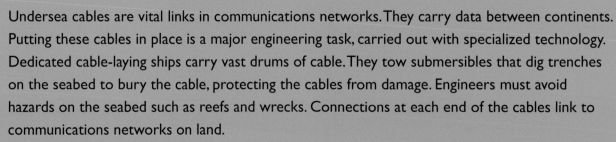

OUT OF CURIOSITY

About 97% of Internet traffic (that's data that travels through the Internet) and phone calls are carried by undersea cables.

UNDERSEA CABLES

Undersea cables are vital links in communications networks. They carry data between continents. Putting these cables in place is a major engineering task, carried out with specialized technology. Dedicated cable-laying ships carry vast drums of cable. They tow submersibles that dig trenches on the seabed to bury the cable, protecting the cables from damage. Engineers must avoid hazards on the seabed such as reefs and wrecks. Connections at each end of the cables link to communications networks on land.

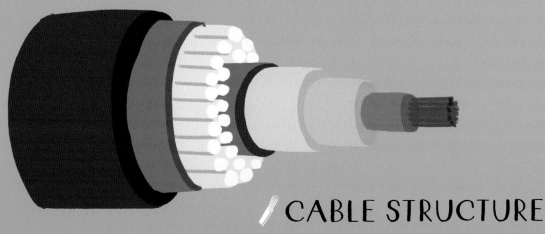

CABLE STRUCTURE

In a data cable, the signals that carry the data are flashes of light that travel along thin glass strands called optic fibers. In an undersea cable, these fragile strands are protected by layers of materials that strengthen and waterproof the cable. The cable is about as thick as a soda can. The signals gradually lose strength, so every 100 km (60 mi) or so, there is a device called a repeater that boosts their strength. Cables normally last about 25 years before they need to be replaced.

SATELLITE ENGINEERING

Communications satellites in orbit relay signals around Earth. They detect signals sent from ground stations and send signals back to other ground stations. Satellite communications are useful in very remote areas of the world and at sea. Electronic engineering also helps to build GPS, remote sensing, and weather satellites.

Our phones work because they connect to a complex telecommunications network that handles calls and data. Telecommunications engineers design, build, and maintain these networks, including the aerial masts that we see dotted around towns, cities, and the countryside.

COMMUNICATIONS MASTS

The aerials on cellular masts send and receive signals from phones. Masts operate within an area called a cell. Mast aerials deal with calls and data for phones in that cell. If you move from one cell to another, the network automatically swaps your phone's signals to the new cell's mast. The cells are smaller in cities than in the countryside to deal with the higher concentration of phones. Masts are linked to each other to make up the phone network. Engineers design masts to stand up to strong winds, then install aerials on them. The aerials must be placed high up, so that signals have a clear route to and from phones on the ground.

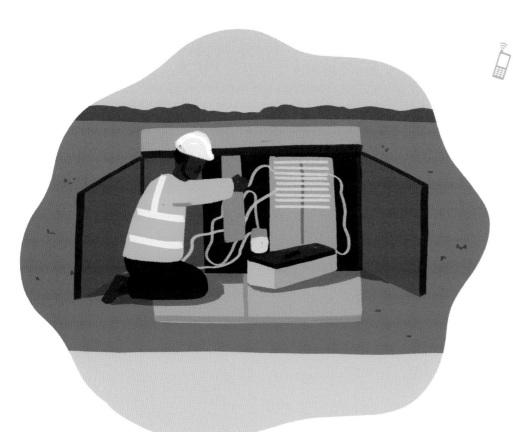

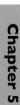 CABLE CONNECTIONS

Most homes, offices, and factories are connected to telecommunications networks by underground or overground cables. The cables can carry phone calls, Internet data, or television signals. All the cables from one area are connected to the telecommunications network at junction boxes. Engineers known as field engineers fix any new cables into these boxes and make repairs if there are breakdowns.

REMOTE ENGINEERING

Telecommunications engineers install cables and phone masts to bring communications to remote places, giving people across the globe access to the Internet and phone network. This means planning the best route for cables, the best sites for aerials, then working in remote areas to install the equipment.

INPUTS AND OUTPUTS

Most electronic machines and gadgets receive and supply information. They do this with inputs and outputs. Inputs contain sensors that recognize touch, movement, light, or sound. Outputs can be lights, speakers, and actuators (which make things move). For example, a digital doorbell has a touch-sensitive button as its input and a buzzer as its output.

((•)) LIGHT AND HEAT SENSORS

A light sensor detects brightness. A simple light sensor stops electricity flowing when light falls on it but allows it to flow when it's dark. This kind of sensor is used in a streetlight to switch it on at night and off during the day. Security lights and alarm systems contain **infrared** (heat) sensors rather than visible-light sensors. The sensor detects the heat coming from a person's body, and the electronic circuits use this to switch on the light for a few seconds or activate an alarm.

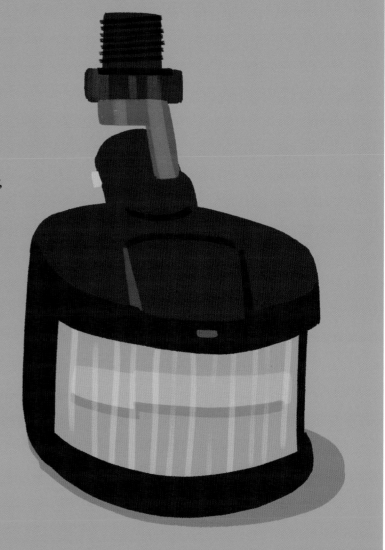

ACTUATORS

An **actuator** is an output device that turns signals from an electronic circuit into motion. A **servo** is a type of electric motor that's often used in remote-controlled models. Signals from a circuit make the wheel move into a particular position or turn at a certain speed. Engineers use electric, **hydraulic**, and **pneumatic** actuators to move the parts of many machines, from aircraft undercarriages to automatic package-sorting machines.

OPTICAL INDICATORS

Information displays made up of **LEDs** are examples of outputs. A single LED might show that a device such as a smoke sensor is switched on or off, or that it's working properly. A grid of LEDs might display numbers, like the display on a digital clock, or be used to show a scrolling message. The LEDs are controlled by electronic circuits in the gadget. A phone or tablet screen is also an optical output made up of millions of tiny LED lights.

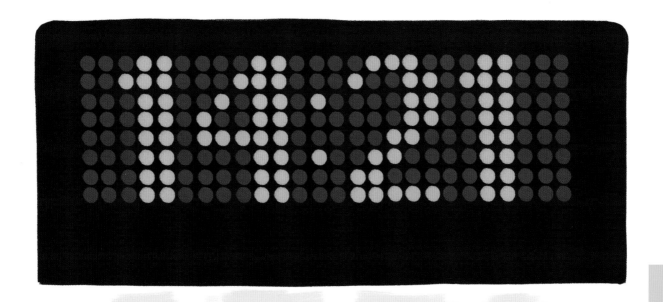

MECHATRONICS

Mechatronics is mechanical engineering and electrical engineering working together. It involves using electronics to control machines such as robot lawn mowers and factory robots. These machines normally have their own on-board computers that are programmed to make them do their jobs.

FACTORY ROBOTS

A robot is a machine that does a job automatically without human help. Most robots are mechanical arms that work in factories, especially in car-making plants. These robots are programmed to repeat complicated movements and fitted with tools such as grippers, drills, soldering irons, and paint sprayers. Sensors detect the position of the joints, and **actuators** move the joints.

WALKING MACHINES

Walking seems like an easy activity for us, but designing a robot that walks on two legs without falling over is a huge challenge for engineers. However, engineers have managed to create robots that can walk, run, and even stay upright when pushed. A walking robot contains dozens of sensors that detect the angle of its joints, the tilt of its body, and how quickly it is falling one way or the other. The robot's computer program uses this data to operate the **actuators** that move the joints, so that the robot moves and keeps its balance. This process is repeated hundreds of times a second to make the robot move smoothly.

⌐ MECHATRONICS IN THE AIR

Mechatronics is useful not only on the ground
but also in the air. **Drones** are robot flying machines that guide
themselves or are remote-controlled. On-board sensors detect
the drone's tilt and position in the air. The on-board computer
calculates how fast to turn each propeller to make the drone fly
in the right direction, at the right speed, and climb or descend.
Mechatronics is also used in aircraft autopilot systems, which
automatically move the aircraft's control surfaces (rudder,
ailerons, and elevators) to keep the plane straight and level.

MEDICAL ELECTRONICS

Electrical and electronic engineers help design and build electrical and electronic machines and devices used in medicine. These can be as simple as digital thermometers or hearing aids, or as complex as body scanners. They also include devices fitted inside patients' bodies, such as pacemakers and replacement joints.

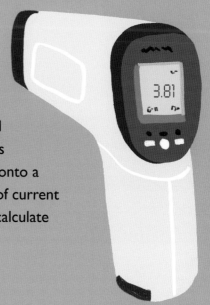

INPUTS AND OUTPUTS

A digital thermometer is an example of a simple medical device that relies on electronic engineering. It uses a lens to focus infrared heat coming from a patient's forehead onto a sensor called a **thermopile**. This changes the amount of current flowing in a circuit inside the thermometer. Electronics calculate the person's temperature and display it on the screen.

MEDICAL SENSORS

A medical monitor measures a patient's vital signs, such as temperature, heart rate, breathing rate, blood pressure, and oxygen levels in the blood. Each sign is measured with a different sensor (these sensors are inputs), and the readings are displayed on a monitor. The sensors work in different ways. For example, the heart-rate sensor detects tiny electrical signals from the heart muscles and the oxygen-level monitor detects how much light the blood absorbs. You might have a fitness monitor with similar sens

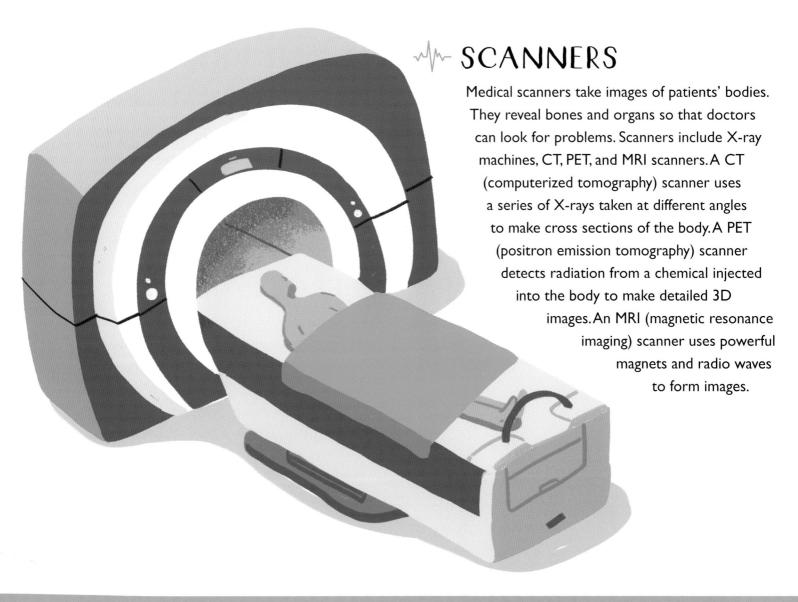

⌁ SCANNERS

Medical scanners take images of patients' bodies. They reveal bones and organs so that doctors can look for problems. Scanners include X-ray machines, CT, PET, and MRI scanners. A CT (computerized tomography) scanner uses a series of X-rays taken at different angles to make cross sections of the body. A PET (positron emission tomography) scanner detects radiation from a chemical injected into the body to make detailed 3D images. An MRI (magnetic resonance imaging) scanner uses powerful magnets and radio waves to form images.

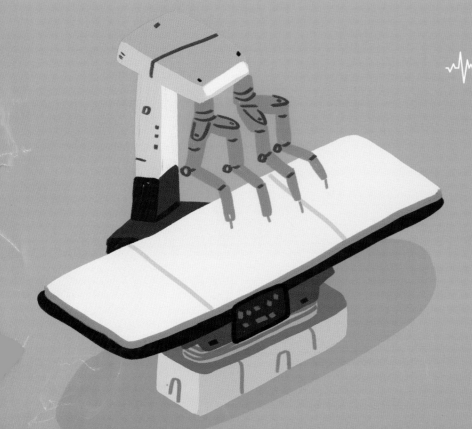

⌁ MEDICAL ROBOTICS

At the cutting edge of medical engineering are surgical robots. These machines assist surgeons with delicate operations. The robot has several arms that hold surgical instruments or cameras, and it can position them with extreme accuracy. A surgeon controls the robot remotely, even from another room or hospital.

SOFTWARE ENGINEERING

Many electronic gadgets and machines, including phones, tablets, computers, robots, and even kitchen appliances such as washing machines and dishwashers, work by following computer programs (software). Designing these programs is called software engineering.

PROGRAMMING

Software engineers figure out what the programs in machines or gadgets need to do. Then, they design the software, which means figuring out exactly how it will work. For complex machines, they might divide the software into sections, each with a job. Computer programmers then write the actual programs. The engineers test the software to check it does what it's supposed to do and make improvements if they are needed.

ARTIFICIAL INTELLIGENCE

With some clever programming by software engineers, machines can appear to think like humans—this is known as artificial intelligence (AI). Machines with artificial intelligence, such as electronic assistants, can do things like recognize human speech and have a conversation with you.

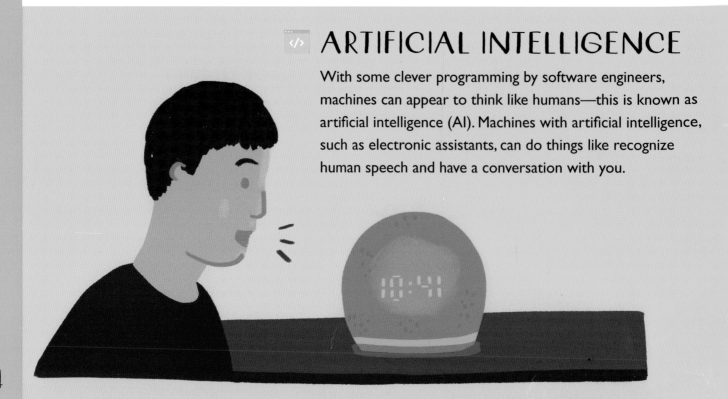

AI FOR GAMES

Artificial intelligence is vital in computer games. The software in many games uses AI to make computer-controlled opponents act in an intelligent way, and as a result they are difficult to beat. Chess was one of the first games that software engineers programmed computers to play. Chess-playing programs are now intelligent enough to beat the world's best chess players.

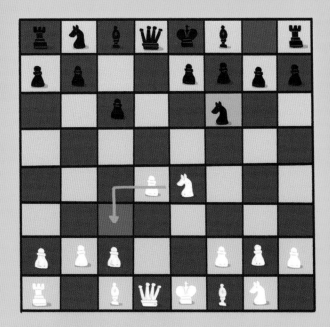

OUT OF CURIOSITY

The first chess-playing computer to beat a world-champion chess player was called Deep Blue. It checkmated Garry Kasparov in 1996.

AI ON THE ROAD

Artificial intelligence plays an important part in prototype self-driving cars. The software that controls the car is very complex. It takes data from the many sensors on the car and decides how to steer the car, speed it up, or slow it down. It must recognize other vehicles and pedestrians on the road and avoid them. It also needs to navigate to its destination.

CHAPTER 6

CHEMICAL ENGINEERING

Chemical engineers design, build, and run chemical plants, where cleaning products, fertilizers, and fuels are produced. They are expert chemists as well as engineers.

In this chapter, you can find out how chemical plants work. Then, we'll look at some other types of engineering linked with chemistry, such as food engineering, agricultural engineering, and biochemical engineering.

CHEMICAL PLANTS

Some chemicals, such as rock salt, we simply dig up and use, but most chemicals are manufactured in factories called chemical plants. The plant turns ingredients (called feedstock chemicals) into the chemicals we need. The design and operation of chemical plants is known as process engineering.

CHEMICAL PRODUCTS

Thousands of different chemicals come out of chemical plants. These include: chemicals used in the home, such as cleaning products and cooking ingredients; chemicals for farmers, such as fertilizers; chemicals for builders, such as cement and paints; and chemicals used in hospitals, such as oxygen.

PLANT DESIGN

The first stage in designing a new chemical plant is to test the chemical process in a laboratory to make sure it works. The process might involve many stages—heating and cooling chemicals, mixing chemicals, reacting chemicals together, and separating chemicals. Then, a chemical engineer draws a "process flow" diagram that shows the various containers (called vessels) needed, the connections between them, and machinery such as pumps and valves. The vessels might contain solids, liquids, or gases, sometimes at very high pressures and temperatures.

A PROTOTYPE PLANT

The next stage in the design involves building a small-scale prototype of the chemical plant called a pilot plant. Engineers test the pilot plant to make sure that everything works as planned. Then, they can design the full-scale plant. They use 3D computer software to visualize how all the vessels and pipes will fit together. Finally, work begins on the full-scale plant. This will involve electrical, mechanical, and structural engineers, as well as chemical engineers.

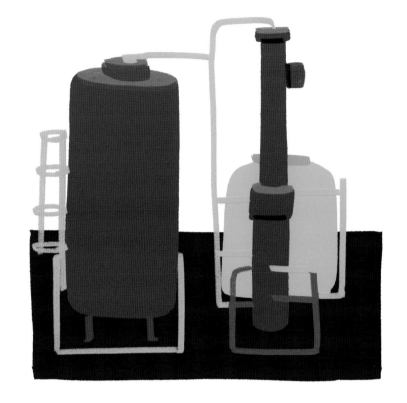

CHEMICAL STORAGE

Chemical plants have storage containers to store feedstock chemicals and products from the plant. These are large enough to store enough chemicals to keep the plant running. Oil refineries have large storage units in an oil depot or tank farm. Some chemicals are stored under pressure in strong spherical containers.

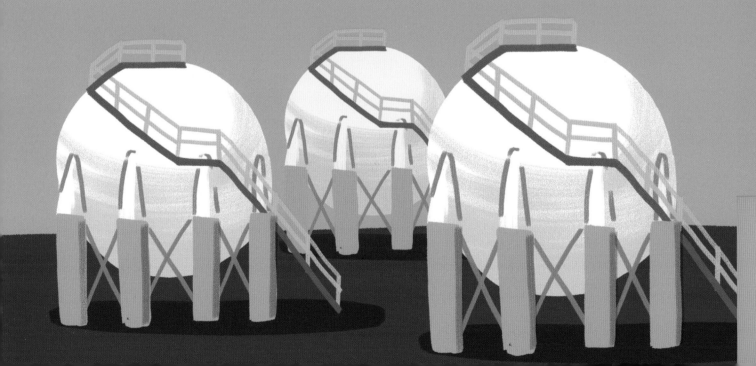

CHEMICAL PLANT OPERATION

Once a new chemical plant has been built and tested, it goes "online" and begins to produce chemicals. A team of engineers operates the plant, making sure it is working safely and efficiently. Engineers also maintain and repair the plant.

 ## PROCESS CONTROL

Engineers monitor how a modern chemical plant is working from a control room. Sensors around the plant measure the temperature of chemicals, the pressure and levels of chemicals in vessels, and how fast liquids and gases are flowing through pipes. This data is fed to the control room and displayed on screens. Engineers can control pumps and valves from the control room. This is known as process control. Computer monitors can display diagrams of the plant for the engineers to view. Finally, closed-circuit television screens allow the engineers to see what's happening around the plant.

PLANT SAFETY

Many of the chemicals produced or stored at a chemical plant are hazardous—they might be inflammable or toxic. Operating a plant safely is important to protect workers and people nearby. Engineers check for problems such as blocked valves or rusty vessels and pipework. Accidents are rare but do happen, leading to fires, explosions, and chemical spills. Plants always have emergency response plans in place.

CHEMICAL TRANSPORTATION

Feedstock chemicals must be delivered to chemical plants, while products and waste are taken away. Chemicals are transported in tanker trucks, tank cars (rail wagons), and ships, and along pipelines. Large volumes of chemicals (called bulk loads) are carried in tanks. Smaller quantities are moved in drums or bottles. Gases, such as propane, are stored in pressurized tankers. The pressure makes them turn to liquid, so they take up less space.

THE OIL AND GAS INDUSTRIES

Chemical engineers, mechanical engineers, and civil engineers
work alongside petroleum engineers in the oil and gas industries.
Together, these engineers help to extract oil and gas from underground
(or under the seabed), transport them to oil refineries, and extract useful
chemicals from them. This is a huge engineering operation.

DRILLING

Oil and gas are found in the rocks of Earth's crust.
Engineers (drilling engineers and production engineers)
operate drilling rigs that bore holes into the rock, first
to search for oil and gas, then to extract it to bring it
to the surface. They work alongside geologists and
other scientists. Many engineers work on offshore
oil platforms.

DRILL BIT

REFINING AND PROCESSING

The oil that's extracted from rocks is known as crude oil or petroleum.
It's a mixture of many different substances called **hydrocarbons**.
These include butane, gasoline (petrol), diesel, kerosene, fuel oil, and
bitumen. The oil is split up into these different parts at an oil refinery,
which is a giant chemical plant. The main process at a refinery is called
distillation—the oil is heated up, and the different parts turn to
gas and rise up a column to different heights, where they cool and are
collected. Gases, such as butane, are collected at the top of the column,
and thick liquid materials, such as bitumen, are collected at the bottom.
These products are stored before being transported away for use.
Gas is processed, too, to purify it before it is burned as a fuel.

PIPELINES

Large amounts of oil and gas are moved around by pumping them through pipelines. Laying these pipelines is a major engineering task. The pipelines carry crude oil from ports where oil tankers dock in order to ship oil products away. Pipelines also carry oil and gas ashore from oil and gas platforms out at sea, and they transport gas between towns and cities. Most pipelines are buried in trenches and made from connected steel tubes. Pumps and valves control the flow of oil and gas along pipelines.

OUT OF CURIOSITY

The Trans-Alaska Pipeline System carries oil 1,219 km (757 mi) from the north coast to the south coast of Alaska. Engineers built it with bends, so that it can flex during earthquakes.

MATERIALS ENGINEERING

Materials engineers develop, test, and manufacture new materials for other engineers to use—perhaps a new metal alloy or a new type of composite material. They also work with existing materials to improve their properties.

MATERIAL PROPERTIES

Engineers have a huge range of materials to choose from, each with different mechanical, electrical, thermal, or chemical properties. Drink cans are made from aluminum because it can be rolled until it's very thin. The lid is pressed so that the aluminum is even thinner around the opening, so that it splits along a line when you pull the ring.

PLASTICS

Plastics and composite materials, such as carbon-reinforced plastic, are commonly being used in place of more traditional materials, such as metals and wood. There are two main types of plastics: **thermoplastics** and **thermosetting** plastics. Thermoplastics melt when they are heated. Thermoplastic beads can be melted and injected into a cast to make objects. Thermosetting plastics are made from runny resin that sets when a chemical called a hardener is added to it. Materials engineers are improving plastic materials all the time, making them lighter and stronger. This is especially important in vehicles and aircraft, where lightness is a great advantage because it saves fuel.

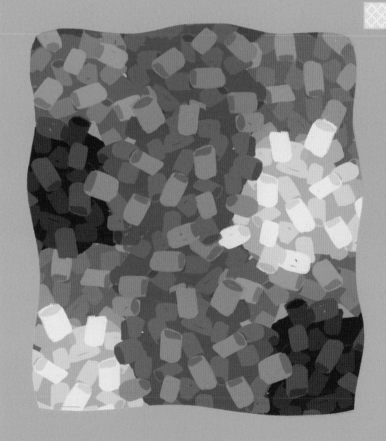

THROUGH THE MICROSCOPE

Engineers study materials to understand their chemical and physical structures. A metal or **alloy** can be studied by making a thin slice of it, polishing the slice, and viewing it under a microscope. This shows up the individual crystals that make up the metal or alloy. The pattern and size of crystals can affect the material's strength. By changing how the material is made or shaped, the crystal size and shape can be changed, improving its strength. This is vital where materials are put under great stress, such as in jet engines.

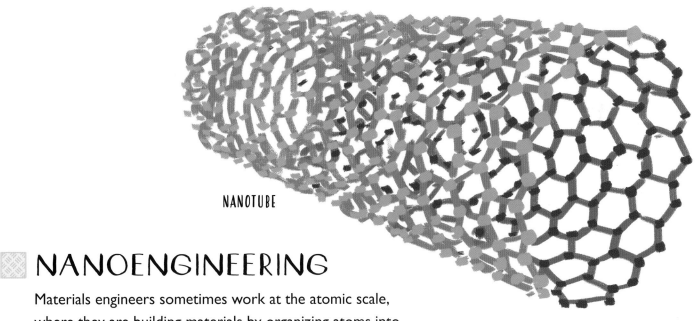

NANOTUBE

NANOENGINEERING

Materials engineers sometimes work at the atomic scale, where they are building materials by organizing atoms into three-dimensional shapes. This is known as nanoengineering, and it's used to make hollow tubes (such as carbon **nanotubes**), fibers, rods, and sheets that are less than one-thousandth the width of a human hair. These materials have many uses, including adding strength to fabrics and composite materials, filtering liquids, and cleaning up toxins.

FOOD ENGINEERING

Applying engineering skills to producing the food we eat is called food engineering. It involves developing new varieties of plants that we get food from, processing plants to make food ingredients, storing food, and producing food in factories.

GENETIC ENGINEERING

Many of the crops we eat have been engineered to grow quickly or be resistant to disease. All plants (and animals) contain a super-complex chemical called DNA that controls how they grow. Every type of plant has different DNA, which makes the plant unique. In genetic engineering, parts of the DNA from one plant are put into the DNA of another plant. This gives the second plant some of the characteristics of the first plant. Engineers use chemicals to break up DNA and piece it back together. It's engineering on a microscopic scale.

FOOD PRODUCTION

Food engineers design and build production lines where the food we buy in stores is produced or packaged. A production line might have many sections that do a particular job, such as mixing ingredients, baking, cutting, canning, bottling, or packaging, each with its own machinery, such as mixing drums, conveyors, dispensers, and ovens. Electronic systems monitor and control the whole operation.

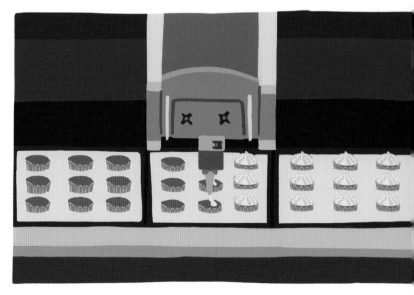

CONTINUOUS LINES

Some types of food, such as cookies, are produced on a production line that runs continuously, twenty-four hours a day. Ingredients are mixed at the start of the line, then a measured amount of dough is dropped onto a wide conveyor belt for each cookie. The conveyor moves slowly through a long oven, so that each cookie spends enough time in the oven to bake perfectly.

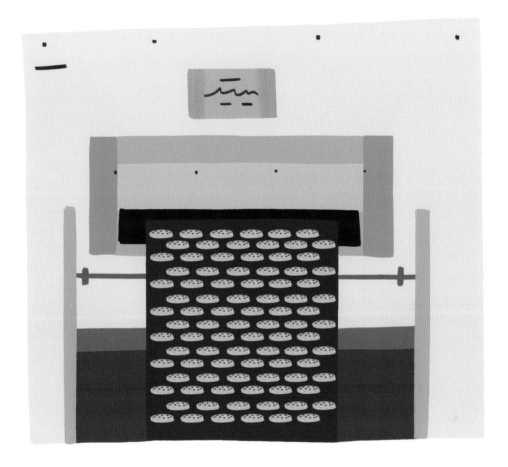

FOOD PACKAGING

Packaging makes food easier to carry and store and helps keep it fresh. Food manufacturers package their food in many materials: cardboard, paper, different types of plastic, metal foil, or combinations of these. Disposable cups are usually made from plastic and cardboard—the plastic is waterproof, while the cardboard is a good **insulator** that keeps the drinks warm. One challenge facing engineers is to make packaging that's 100% recyclable.

BIOCHEMICAL ENGINEERING

Biochemistry is the science that studies the chemistry that happens in living things. Biochemical engineering is a mixture of chemistry, biology, and engineering. Biochemical engineers use biological processes inside plant and animal cells to make chemicals used in medical drugs and washing powders.

DRUG DEVELOPMENT

Many chemicals in drugs—such as antibiotics, which fight infections, and vaccines, which keep you from catching diseases—are made using biochemical engineering. Biochemical engineers change the way that cells (from plants, animals, bacteria, or algae) work to make the cells produce the chemicals we need. Developing a new drug is a very long process, but the stages are similar to the stages of design in other branches of engineering. The drug must be thoroughly tested in clinical trials before it is allowed to be used.

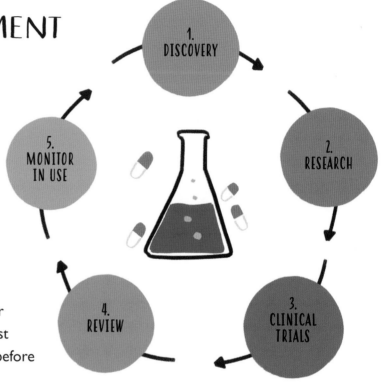

1. DISCOVERY
2. RESEARCH
3. CLINICAL TRIALS
4. REVIEW
5. MONITOR IN USE

BIOFUELS

In our fight against global warming, we need to reduce the amount of fossil fuels (oil, gas, and coal) that we use. Algal biofuels are one of the alternatives being developed by biochemical engineers. An algal biofuel is a fuel produced by algae (seaweed and the green stuff that grows on ponds). Engineers have had success with this method in the laboratory, but there is a lot of research to do before the process will work on a large scale.

BIO FIRST AID

Biochemical engineers have developed materials called **hydrogels**. These are made up of **polymers**, which themselves are made up of many small molecules joined together to make long chains. Hydrogels may contain lots of water. Hydrogels made from natural polymers (such as a chemical called collagen) using biochemical engineering are used as burn and wound dressings. Similar technology is being used in the development of tissue engineering, which could lead to engineers being able to grow replacement human organs.

FOOD PRODUCTION

Biochemical engineering is used widely in the food industry to process food. Even a simple loaf of bread makes use of biochemistry. Most types of bread are made to rise using yeast, which is a type of fungus. The yeast feeds on sugars to make carbon dioxide, which creates bubbles inside the bread. Biochemical engineers have engineered yeasts to make them work more quickly. They have also developed preservatives that make the bread last for longer.

ON THE FARM

Agricultural engineering is the use of engineering in farming. Chemical engineering is vital for farmers: Chemical plants produce fertilizers, pesticides, and foodstuffs for animals. Biochemical engineers develop new crop species that produce more food, and mechanical engineers design and build machinery.

FERTILIZERS

Fertilizers are one of the major products from chemical plants. Fertilizers contain minerals such as nitrates, phosphates, and sulfates that plants need to grow. Plants grow more quickly when fertilizer is added to the soil. Fertilizers are made in stages. To make a common fertilizer called ammonium nitrate, first nitrogen is extracted from the air and reacted with hydrogen to make ammonia. The ammonia is used to make nitric acid, which in turn is used to make the ammonium nitrate.

SPRAYING CHEMICALS

Farmers also use pesticides and herbicides, which are both produced at chemical plants. Pesticides kill plants, insects, and other animals that damage crops by feeding on them, but they don't damage the crops themselves. Herbicides are pesticides that prevent weeds from growing among the crops and using up valuable nutrients. Insecticides are pesticides that kill insects. Other chemicals target other animals, bacteria, or fungi.

FARM MACHINERY

Mechanical engineers design and build farm machinery—machinery for preparing and treating the soil with fertilizers, sowing seeds, watering and harvesting crops, and transportation. Engineers are producing robot machines that do some of these jobs automatically, steered by GPS and other sensors. A weeding robot removes unwanted plants very accurately without damaging the crops.

FOREST ENGINEERING

Mechanical engineers also design and build machinery for forestry engineering. There are machines for preparing the soil for trees to be planted, for planting saplings, for applying pesticides to protect the young trees, and special machines for harvesting trees, which cut down and strip a tree trunk in one swift operation.

THE WORLD AROUND US

Environmental engineering is using engineering skills to protect and improve the environment. Environmental engineers help provide clean water, control pollution, get rid of waste, and recycle materials. This branch of engineering is becoming more and more important as we try to keep our planet healthy and fix environmental problems from the past.

PROTECTING WATER

Pollution is a problem in rivers, lakes, oceans, and groundwater (water in the soil and rocks under the ground). It comes from farms, human waste, and chemical spills. It affects not only animals and plants that live in the water, but also humans who drink or bathe in the water. Environmental engineers take water samples to test how clean water is. The results tell them if pollution controls are working.

MANAGING WASTE

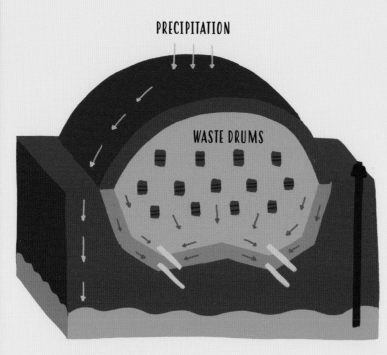

PRECIPITATION

WASTE DRUMS

Some industries, including the chemical industry, produce hazardous waste—solids, liquids, and gases that would be harmful to the planet if they got into the water or the atmosphere. Environmental engineers are involved in burying this dangerous waste in "landfill" sites. Any leaks of dangerous chemicals are prevented by the thick liner, and groundwater around the site is regularly checked for pollution. Domestic waste is put in similar landfill sites. Specialist environmental engineers work in the nuclear industry, dealing with the burial of nuclear waste, which will be hazardous for thousands of years to come.

TREATING WATER

Environmental engineers help manage wastewater from towns and cities. This contains water that has flowed into street drains and dirty water from kitchens and bathrooms. Systems of pipes (called sewers) take the water to treatment plants, where it goes through a series of processes to clean it before it's returned to rivers or the sea.

DISASTER RESPONSE

When environmental disasters such as oil spills happen, environmental engineers help with the response. They look at the site of the accident, what chemicals have been spilled, what plants and animals are affected, and even what weather is expected. Then, they decide the best way to clean up, so that habitats can recover as quickly as possible.

ENGINEERING THE FUTURE

Engineering will always be vital for humans and our planet.
Engineers will continue to make advances in areas such as
communications and medicine. They will also need to find answers
to some of the challenges ahead, such as providing enough water for
growing populations and helping us all become carbon neutral.

FACING CLIMATE CHANGE

Global warming is bringing changes all over our planet, and things will probably get
worse before we can stop the warming. Sea levels are slowly rising, and there are
increasing numbers of severe weather events, such as floods and droughts. Engineers will
help protect areas along coasts and near rivers from flooding, help provide enough clean
water for everyone, and help farmers develop drought-resistant crops.

SUSTAINABLE MATERIALS

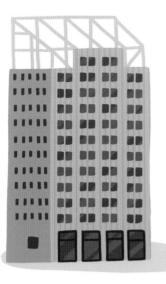

Engineers will need to help us live more sustainable lives by wasting fewer materials. An example already being tried is the use of wooden frames in high-rise building. Wood is a sustainable material since it can be grown naturally and rots away when it's finished with. It can be light and strong and is a more eco-friendly material than steel or concrete because it takes much less energy to make.

RECYCLING FOR ENGINEERING

Living sustainable lives also means throwing away less stuff. Engineers can help us recycle more materials, make things with materials that are easy to recycle, and find ways of reusing stuff. Civil engineers make houses from old shipping containers, which reduces the need for new building materials, waste, and the energy needed to recycle the containers.

ENGINEERING IN SPACE

It may be many years before humans set foot on the planet Mars, but when the day comes, engineers will be there. Over the years, engineers have invented many different types of shelters that could be taken to Mars in sections and assembled on arrival. One of the latest ideas from NASA engineers is a beehive-shaped shelter that would be built from Martian soil using a giant 3D printer.

GLOSSARY

actuator: A device, such as an electric motor, that moves part of a machine.

alloy: A material made by mixing a metal with another material (normally another metal).

aquaplane: To slide across the surface of a layer of water.

axle: A rod that can turn around, normally with a wheel attached to its end.

bionic: Describes an artificial limb such as an arm or leg that is moved by motors.

bit: Part of a milling machine or drill that does the cutting.

brace: Part of a structure or machine that holds the structure or machine in shape.

capacitor: An electronic component that stores electricity.

circuit: A series of electric or electronic components arranged in a ring so that electricity can flow through them.

cofferdam: A temporary, circular dam used when building bridge foundations in water. Water is pumped out from inside the dam.

compression: When a material is squeezed.

conductor: A material that allows electricity to flow through it easily.

corrosion: When a metal is eaten away and weakened by chemicals. Rust on iron is a type of corrosion.

distillation: A way of separating a mixture of different liquids.

ductile: Describes a metal that can be stretched into a thin wire.

dynamo: A device that turns movement into electricity.

elastic: Describes a material that can be stretched, squashed, or bent and then returns to its original shape.

electromagnetic radiation: Rays of energy including light, heat, and radio waves.

geodesic: Describes a dome made from a framework of rods connected in triangles and other regular shapes.

groma: A measuring instrument used by Roman engineers when they built new roads.

hydraulic: When liquid is pumped through pipes to make parts of a machine move.

hydrocarbon: A chemical that contains the elements hydrogen and carbon.

hydrogel: A clear, sticky material that holds water (a bit like a sponge).

infrared: A type of light that is invisible but carries heat.

insulator: A material that stops the flow of electricity or reduces the flow of heat.

isometric view: A type of 3D view of an object.

laminate: A material made by gluing two or more layers of other materials together.

lathe: A tool used to shape a spinning rod of material.

malleable: Describes a metal that can be hammered or pressed into shape without breaking.

nanotube: An extremely thin tube made with carbon atoms.

photolithography: A way of making printing plates using photography.